Managing Abundance:
The Ethics Paradigm

Managing Abundance: The Ethics Paradigm

A Business-like Approach to Demit Scarcity and Admit Abundance

Pradeep Nevatia, scd and Rahul Nevatia

BEP

BUSINESS EXPERT PRESS

Leader in applied, concise business books

Managing Abundance: The Ethics Paradigm: A Business-like Approach to Demit Scarcity and Admit Abundance

Copyright © Business Expert Press, LLC, 2021.

Cover design by Charlene Kronstedt

Interior design by Exeter Premedia Services Private Ltd., Chennai, India

First published in 2021 by
Business Expert Press, LLC
222 East 46th Street, New York, NY 10017
www.businessexpertpress.com

ISBN-13: 978-1-95334-970-5 (paperback)
ISBN-13: 978-1-95334-971-2 (e-book)

Business Expert Press Business Ethics and Corporate Citizenship Collection

Collection ISSN: 2333-8806 (print)
Collection ISSN: 2333-8814 (electronic)

First edition: 2021

10 9 8 7 6 5 4 3 2 1

Dedicated to *Saturnrings'* time principle that approbates *present,* co-terminus with truth.

Description

India's rural BPO guru Pradeep Nevatia joins with New York-based hedge fund investor Rahul Nevatia to present the until-now abstract concept of abundance through an innovative managing by ethics (MBE) framework that uncompromisingly connects individual self to collective self in self-sustained abundance beyond the hocus-pocus of scarcity. As against the card-carrying management by objectives (MBO) acquirement, the pioneering MBE paradigm sets human—nature co-existence as the basis to realize abundance, the source energy of all beings.

The ethics—abundance theme of this book could not be timelier for businesses to reconstruct their growth strategies for a sustainable future following the coronavirus pandemic. The industrial and financial engineering duo has leveraged their respective business turnaround and foot-on-the-gas-pedal backgrounds to thoroughly revamp the contemporary policy—goal deployment methodologies and make determined amendments to reconfigure several management processes in vogue to deliver sustainable business results in a meaningfully restructured leadership—fellowship relationship dynamic replacing the scarcity-driven everyday mill with natural rhythms of abundance.

Keywords

abundance principle; animative speed; balancing motor; cause and effect; coexistence; cognitive speed; collaboration; collective self; common minimum program; competition; consciousness; constancy; contingency; contingent time; corona effect; cosmic energy; creed hierarchy; deserts of alienation; desire fulfillment; destiny; dignity; dis-values; economic motor; economistic; efficiency; empathy motor; end-state values; entropy; equilibrium; ethics–abundance; ethics; abundance; ethics in business; ethics at work; ethics–inertia; ethics paradigm; everyday time; evolution through involution; first thing first; framework for longevity; freedom motor; free will; gaia; gaia system; gaia time; globalization; greed hierarchy; greed maximization; Hawthorne effect; hub and spoke; human flourish; humanistic; humanizing; inertia; intellect; involution; man in human; managing by ethics; managing surprises; Maslow's need hierarchy; maximizer; MBE; MBO; meditating on the go; metric for growth; motivating; Narendra Modi; need hierarchy; need optimization; normative speed; oasis of resonance; ordinate goal; period leader; P-O-L-C; P-O-L-S; productivity karma; quality dharma; quality of mind; resonance; rural BPO; scarcity; self-actualization; self-managed; self-realization; serial leadership; slippery slopes; speed-greed; subjective; superordinate goal; sustainability; think and counter think; three-box solution; timeless time; TQM; troika model; universalization; valuator; value sourcing; value as means; vocal for local; work ethic

Contents

Preface

It is an irony that my first operational turnaround project at Union Carbide's factory in Kashmir Valley coincided with the outset of insurgency in Jammu and Kashmir back in 1989 with mass exodus of Kashmiri Pandits from the valley. As a result, the factory was abandoned, and operations were suspended sine die. I was the head of Industrial Engineering and Operations at the factory. Despite the global standards set by Union Carbide, the factory had a long history of operating at below-par efficiency. However, the relationship between the leadership rank and grassroots workforce was largely cordial, except when it came to delivering efficiency at work! The only tool I had in my learning in those days was my academic knowledge of industrial engineering. I, therefore, deployed my untried and untested knowledge of time and motion studies to examine assembly lines at the factory, admittedly deviating from usual industrial engineering design. My point of interest was not limited to examining the iterative behavior of machines, conveyors, or chutes. I also intended to understand how the man at machine was emotionally reacting and responding to the challenges he was facing to deal with everyday operational issues posed by those machines and auxiliaries. I spent a good 10 hours every day at the factory. But, before I could complete my two-week long study and analyze the data, operational efficiency, which was steadily upping since the beginning of the study, had surpassed the standards set by any of Union Carbide's factories in India by the time the study was completed. It was bit of *Hawthorne effect* of course, but the key takeaway for me was that people matter—and matter the most. Everything else could be impersonalized, but not the human. A human is just her emotion, and surely, there is no dominant difference between one and another, but the variance in the way they emote. Emotion is what actually sets the man in motion and regulates his actions in the direction to fulfill his unfulfilled desires.

Anyway, I was out of the frying pan, possibly with flying colors, but put back on fire once again at another one of Union Carbide's factories—this time in Kolkata, in eastern India. This factory had an interesting organization and work culture. Located in the midst of a highly volatile and charged trade union-driven myth, the workforce was decidedly skilled and largely returned from well-to-do and educated family backgrounds. In other words, they had deep-rooted beliefs, and they believed they knew what ethically–morally was right or wrong. They also knew how to carry out their assigned tasks in the most efficient way. However, fact remained that barring the early few years since its inception, operations were inefficient and employee relations were largely discordant at most times. As the head of the wage negotiation committee, I had to deal with people who knew more about operations than me—however, I knew more about my ignorance than they knew about theirs! And here was the catch—in the mill of the greed–speed grind, a man gets so fixated to his individualistic desire-fulfillment agenda that he tends to ignore, to his own peril, the collective need-fulfillment purpose that he himself could be a part of. To cut a long story short, for the first time in the factory's history, an agreement was signed between the heretofore warring factions to serve and fulfill a common and collective agenda, and a formula was arrived at, to share the impending gains between the two parties. This was September 1996. As the head of factory by then, I fondly recall the celebrations that commemorated the best productivity milestone ever achieved by the factory. This was the authority of collectivism!

A similar situation brewed up down in southern India in Chennai, in 1999. This was the Indian arm of a U.S.-based company, albeit in the yet-to-mature space of information technology enabled services (ITES). With a no-holds-barred focus on recovering the investment made, the company's leadership flock solely targeted new account wins and pushed shipments and deliveries to the maximum—every hour on each day. This was Taylorism at its waning least—crawling and clambering even in service and support industries—who is who in the organization was in all likelihood known only to the clients—to none in the organization! Eventually, things started falling apart, the company was practically business-sick and all set to close. This was the time I assumed the role as the chief executive officer (CEO) of the company with more than 7,500 employees and contractors. Being new to ITES, I knew no better than to take the reserve of some proven manufacturing principles to the work theater, customize them, and roll them out. One by one, such systems and methods were introduced—total quality management (TQM) and ISO standards compliance, the concept of statistical quality control sufficing a *virtual manufacturing environment*, and the like. But the most crucial intervention was to place the employee actor at the center of all business episodes. Everything must serve the actor, and not the other way round. The employee actor must be delighted first to make business patrons delighted, for she could never give more than what she had in her. Finally, the company was not just out of the looming threat of closure but went on to introduce pioneering concepts like rural BPO (2005) and college campus BPO (2005) for the industry. Each employee actor was made part of a team and encouraged to contribute her unique expertise for the collective agenda. No one had to work for more than stipulated hours. Such a concept of "work-life balance" might be as plain as a pikestaff following a pandemic "work-from-home" year, but it was surprisingly unique back then. Business and family times were guardedly balanced out and appropriately proportionated. It was a large team spread over several branch offices in Chennai, but all were united by a common mission—be happy first and pass it on the next. Latterly, as a hugely profitable business, the company changed hands with another ITES venture, and I moved on to yet another firm on a ventilator in an intensive care unit!

This was a call center company in Chennai I took charge of in early 2010, with an idea to possibly pull it out of its imminent closure. On the very first day of assuming office, I was confronted with a list of 800 employees on the firing line. Here was a situation that was in a way a combination of all the three previous situations I narrated. My approach here was also a mix of the three in tandem. Among the first things done was to intermit the *IT way* of the parent company and install the *BPO way* to manage the affairs of a BPO business. The troika structure, which we shall discuss in the following pages, was introduced to align the disjointed leadership huddle to a common purpose—and all the needless tasks were summarily eliminated forthwith. Although several analytical tools and techniques were deployed to take decisions with *detached attachment*, the basic thrust was to foster an environment in which the employee actors could breathe freely and establish their individual identity within a collective identity. By March 2014, the company had spread its operations across multiple locations in the country, serving across multiple business verticals and recorded its first profitable year. Employee attrition and absenteeism were at lowest levels versus the industry benchmarks—the employee actors were movingly happy!

Of course, the world of business is full of many such stories and many successful turnarounds, but we have un-crated here in this book the ideas and concepts culled from these experiences to map out—an until-now abstract—the subject of subjectivity into a thoroughly reconstructed objective framework emerging straight from gemba, the live workplace. Man with a scarcity mind misses the universe of abundance completely and sees only a limited world with limited possibilities. Abundance, the very source of all beings and things, beyond the realm of the mind, must, therefore, be realized within the self itself—for all space and time are integral within the inner abundance, the primary basis of man's inner-world sustainability and outer-world maintainability. Rahul Nevatia, my co-author, with his unique experience at New York hedge funds, has added the missing west perspective in the north, east, and south perspective I have described, synthesizing a complete 360-degree bearing to the ethics–abundance narrative of the book—and in this full circle, we are placing the man in an organization without omission and in human by commission!

We have deliberately included an unusually large number of illustrations in this book to expound the hitherto esoteric subjective in a rather audible and objective way. Subjectivity could only be experienced by way of objectivity—therefore, the illustrations and depictions could be incredibly supportive to an intricate dissertation. During the course of our work, we have referenced some outstanding books, particularly by Harmut Rosa, Michael Pirson, Vijay Govindarajan, S. K. Chakraborty, and A. Parthasarathy. These books were quite pertinent to how we constructed our arguments and the narrative of this book. We sincerely express our gratitude to these eminent thinkers and authors. We also thank many other illustrious humans who have shaped our thoughts and actions through the course of our work life in past several years. And, of course, our avid and ardent gratitude is to Prof. David Wasieleski, Executive Director, Institute of Ethics in Business at Duquesne University, United States, to guide us through to writing this book—his interventions and suggestions were of immense value to us—yes, the egg in our bear! Finally, I thank my wife Sangita for so graciously allowing me the liberty with time even in the midst of coronavirus lockdowns. And, I am sure, Rahul, my co-author, must be equally thankful to his wife, Preeti, and his spirited kids, Aarav and Anishka, for similar generosity from them as well.

Pradeep Nevatia, scd
Chennai, Kolkata, New York

Foreword

The world is experiencing a multitude of converging crises that force us to rethink how we manage and lead. The situation we find ourselves in forces us to take a new look. We are called to question our notions of reality and ourselves. Managing Abundance guides us to do both.

Let me then set out to writing this foreword with exhortation that the book you now hold in your hands has the cogency and potency to unmask the camouflaged you within the emergent making of a business and society. The book does not only edify but also creates momentum on how people and organizations can take stock of what is happening around them and seek to reset their lives and livelihoods. The work presented stems from practical insights of real live managers and investor and complements many of the emerging insights from theory on how we can manage ourselves and others better.

In this book the authors shed light on the possibility of organizing life around the principle of abundance. This principle is labeled the ethical code of universal consciousness that perpetuates the unbiased and collective human flourishing agenda of humanity—individual happiness as intrinsic within it. They will walk you through how you can create the construct of ethics–abundance for a perpetual business organization that could last a "100 years." They will demonstrate how deeply rooted the idea of scarcity is in our mind and how it can drive us into a greed–speed frenzy and onto the slippery slopes of individualistic agenda.

The author duo carries a comprehensive analytical and business background—Pradeep is a former CEO of large people-intensive companies and Rahul is a hedge fund investor. One is deeply involved with people and the other is so with numbers. Diligent and intensive effort by these authors reflects in the strength of book's ethics–abundance theme qualified through their exclusive subjective-objective narrative. They have brought a kind of distinctive economistic–humanistic perspective, so to say, to the "abstract" concept of abundance by way of a well-argued ethics paradigm. This book should be given to every CXO, so that they can realize the opportunities in a seemingly chaotic world. The authors do an excellent job showing in illustrative detail just how easy it is to strengthen the foundation of a "sustainable" business framework.

This is not a book for those who are afraid to tread undiscovered paths! This is a book for those who dare to see beyond the individualistic economic goals into the collective human mission. And this is not a "lazy in-flight reading" book. This is a "break out to self-discovery" book. Go forth, reader, and learn of the vitality of self-sustained abundance and its innate ethics code!

Michael Pirson
Professor and President, International Humanistic
Management Association
New York, 2021

PART I

The Perspective

CHAPTER 1

Man in Human: The Scarcity in Abundance

Managing the Manager

Some 40 years ago, Professor B. S. Rao, during a system dynamics discussion at the National Institute of Industrial Engineering, Mumbai, described "manager as the one who could manage at least one person other than herself." We overwhelmingly subscribe to this, albeit with one adaptation that is exceptional in prevailing times. It is exigent upon us to explicitly introduce the inseparable man–nature relationship extension to the definition of the manager even if it were implicit in the definition originally put forward by the professor. In an altered definition of the manager, therefore, we would like to elucidate the description of a manager as the one who could manage at least one person other than herself and her *gaia self*. We have borrowed the phrase *Gaia* from Greek mythology in which the primordial earth, including its ecosphere and biosphere, is characterized as gaia. We consider that the hitherto embedded gaia-element of human existence must be separated out and given unambiguous assiduity and latitude in any disquisition over the inside-out dynamics of not just the manager, but the man-in-human system itself at both subjective as well as objective planes. The core of managing is management of first the human—her unlimited subjective self, and then, the man—his limited objective self. The effect commensurate only with its cause, no matter the system. This is the fundamental cause–effect principle. Therefore, how objective affairs of the world outside are managed reflects just how subjective affairs of the man within are managed. And, no discussion about the man-in-business could, therefore, be complete without a corresponding deliberation on man-in-human in its object–subject dynamics and finite–infinite dimension, that is to say, the limited in unlimited—the scarcity in abundance.

Energy: The Matter of Time

In physical sciences, as we know, the relationship between energy, matter and time is explained through Einstein's famous equation: $E = MC^2$, where E is energy, M is matter, and C is the time dimension that expresses energy—potential and kinetic—in terms of speed of light. We are, of course, not going into the physics per se of this equation, but picking up our key takeaway from here, that for any dynamic—animate or inanimate cosmic system, the three basic constituents are cosmic energy, cosmic matter, and perpetual time. In other words, the cosmic energy on all counts is expressed through matter in the chronicle of time. Also, the energy–matter ratio maintains a holistic balance or the constancy over a perpetual and therefore the infinite time dimension between the minus and plus infinities conjoined in circularity. Cosmic energy—kinetic and potential—expresses itself, in form through matter and in movement through time. This is what a cosmic system or within that the gaia system is at its grossest level of manifestation. We are of course not going into any inquiry as to how cosmic energy came into being and what caused the cosmic energy to express itself as cosmic matter along this perpetual time dimension. Although through epochs, different religious thoughts have explained this phenomenon in different ways, we call this an interplay of—uncaused, undifferentiated, unfragmented, and unitive—energy with matter and time and leave it at that to continue further into developing our postulations. This otherwise attribute-less cosmic energy or to use the philosophical paraphrase, the consciousness has a four-dimensional being character:

1. It is *self-sustained* in abundance as against to-be-managed in scarcity.
2. It is *integrative* and unitive.
3. It is *infinite* and perennial.
4. It is *rhythmic* in a sort of sinusoidal movement.

The first two dimensions pertain to its subjective character, and the latter two pertain to the objective character. We shall discuss further the character of cosmic energy in relevant contexts during the course of our deliberations in the following pages of this book.

The Being Principle of Scarcity and Abundance

Cosmic energy, as we get, is uncaused; therefore, it is self-determined, self-sustained, and self-abiding in its own existence principle—we call the abundance principle. Vedantic philosophy calls it the *perpetual dharma*, the holding principle, or the ethics principle. The word dharma comes from the Sanskrit root—dhri, which means to hold or to support. Therefore, dharma stands for the substratum that holds or supports the determination and sustenance of a thing or being. In other words, the abundance principle, as we call it, holds, supports, and sustains the collective consciousness—the unitive cosmic energy—of the integrated human. We could say, the abundance principle sustains the undifferentiated and infinite energy, which in turn is expressed though differentiated matter over the finite chronicle of time. We shall use the terms abundance principle and ethics principle interchangeably in our discussions all through this book. The same argument, therefore, could also be extended to explain the idea of scarcity maxim or the individual dharma. The scarcity maxim holds, supports, and manages the differentiated man in individual consciousness. The individual being—the man—is, therefore, the manifestation of collective being—the human. Individual consciousness established in individual principle is what an individual being is. We shall, therefore, refer abundance principle in the context of human in collective consciousness and scarcity maxim in the context of man in individual consciousness. In this sense, the abundance principle is the *collective principle* as well.

Moving on further, the man-in-human system is said to be congruent when both individual consciousness and collective consciousness are perfectly aligned. Each and everything or being in the cosmos is, thus, a combination of objectivity and subjectivity in varied proportion and multiple permutation and combination. Moreover, human is the only subject–object being in the gaia system who has access to her complete subject–object dimension of cosmic expression—the animals, birds, trees, and so on do not have the subjective dimension. Therefore, to understand the *total human system* and how it interacts with the beings and steers through the gaia system, we need to understand both the subjective and objective dimensions of human personality.

The Being Consciousness: Human Personality Planes

For the greatest part, as we know, a human being is constituted of a physical body, a mind, and an intellect. The body–mind–intellect system is the matter that, by itself, is inert and inanimate just as for any other living being. The five organs of perception in human body take in the stimuli from the world. Mind and intellect react with the stimuli and direct the organs of action in the human body to send out commensurate response back into the world. If the mind alone reacts to the stimuli—without engagement with the intellect—there is a particular response that is just mind-directed—according to the nature of mind, and if body–mind–intellect combine reacts to the stimuli, the response bears the characteristics of intellect as well. For the time being, we are putting on hold—for a later stage examination—a third possibility when intellect alone could respond by bypassing the mind and proceed further to discuss how the body–mind–intellect system is functionally organized within the overall human system and how it coordinates its contingent functionality.

As we know, our concept of objects in the outer world is gained only through the five sense organs secured in the human physical body. If these sense organs are inactive, there is no world for the man, or in other words, it is existent as nullity. The human body forms the grossest encumbrance of the manifested cosmic energy. The objective sense in turn is connected with the subjective sense through the five planes of human existence or human personality planes, progressively subtler than the previous, see Figure 1.1.

1. Animative plane: This is the plane of physical body—the outermost precinct of human personality—beyond which man has no physical existence. It essentially emerges out from the assimilated food and finally goes back to fertilize the earth matter and becomes the food itself. Therefore, the physical body is an integrated bio-gaia body separately identifiable only in the finite timeframe of man's limited lifetime. The bio and gaia bodies comprise the same core elements and mutually impact each other like the sub-system within the system. The animative plane comprises of the organs of action and the five organs of perception that connect it to adjoining planes of human personality.

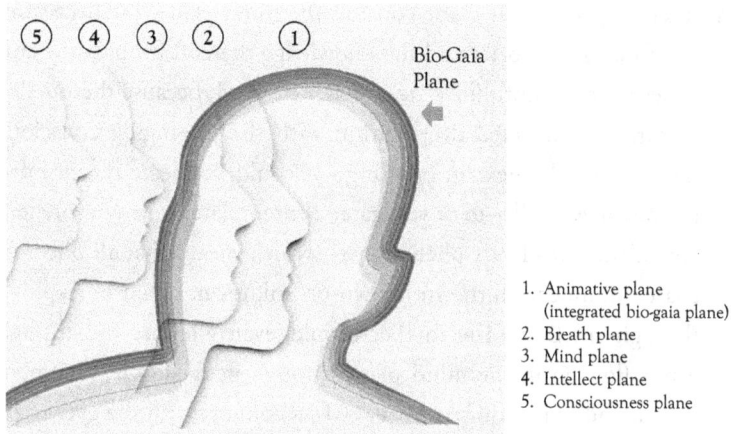

1. Animative plane
   (integrated bio-gaia plane)
2. Breath plane
3. Mind plane
4. Intellect plane
5. Consciousness plane

Bio-Gaia Plane

Figure 1.1 Human personality planes

2. Breath plane: This is the plane of five psychological systems comprising the faculties of perception, digestion, blood circulation, thinking, and self-learning. The medium running through these five faculties of human psychological personality is the dynamic air or, as we call, the pulse of breath. This is also plane of balance between the animative (action) plane and the adjoining mind (thought) plane and, therefore, pivotal to establish thought–action congruity.

3. Mind plane: This is the plane of the emotional mind that regulates pulses of breath in the breath plane. The emotional mind—or just the mind—comprises a continuous flow of thought pulses and waves of different frequencies. The mind by itself remains within the realm of known or the finites, as its operative signals are primarily drawn from the finite outer world. However, mind is, could as well be, in state of duality for its capacity to simultaneously connect with both objective–finite, the outer and subjective–infinite, the inner worlds of the man. The thought pulses in the mind—emotions or feelings—are, therefore, oscillatory in nature, for they oscillate between the outer objective and inner subjective focal points on the mind plane and the contiguous intellect plane. This also explains the natural propensity of mind to be either in the no-more-valid past—the world of memories and the not-yet-valid future—the world of hopes and wishes—this is the prime essence.

4. Intellect plane: This plane controls the mind plane. Intellect stores all of man's memories and the knowledge thereof. It holds the congeries of man's unfulfilled desires as well. And, because the intellect in turn is connected deep within with the impinging consciousness plane—the next in ordering—it could permeate the realm of unknown as well—to investigate, contemplate, and comprehend any of the out-of-box phenomena—which means that all phenomena or noumena, hitherto known or unknown, could be explored through intellect. The intellect could even alleviate the thought waves flowing in the mind plane through its faculty of judgment, the capability it acquires, by way of its connect with the ever-stable consciousness plane—for judgment, as we know, a stable reference is indispensable.

5. Consciousness plane: This is the innermost of all the five personality planes, which is partially or fully insulated from the being consciousness—the abundance of cosmic energy of man through the layers of his *unfulfilled desires*, collimated in the intellect plane. The desire is an all-important and essential vector phenomenon ($\bar{d}$-fulfillment) of the undifferentiated cosmic energy that causes its manifestation into differentiated matter of specific form and dynamic movement along the direction of its desire-centric propensity. The manifestation of this energy could be dynamic active—kinetic energy—or dynamic passive—potential energy—or in any of their permutation and combination. The consciousness plane directly controls the function of intellect plane through unfulfilled desires accumulated there in that. In other words—we could say—if there is no desire, there is no human—this is the prime essence.

The Cause of Being: Desire Fulfillment

Sir Isaac Newton's *Mathematical Principles of Natural Philosophy* postulates that physical objects or bodies establish an equilibrium through exertion of equal and opposite forces. Extending this principle to man's subjective domain, we could also say that a subjective noumenon could as well establish equilibrium through a set of equal and opposite subjective forces. Desire, being a thought noumenon of man's subjective personality, could, therefore, shape into an action phenomenon only through incidence of equally powerful and opposing thoughts. However, the positive or negative polarity of the force of desire could be referenced only with respect to the orientation of desired goal (desire vector - $\vec{d}$), the mind ports at a particular point of time. The thought current flowing along $\vec{d}$ -fulfillment is considered positive and flowing against is considered negative by the man. In other words—in the anxiety for success ($\vec{d}$ -fulfillment), there is lurking fear of failure ($\vec{d}$ -unfulfillment) concurrent with it in the mind. This pulsating movement of energy from the success to the failure end generates a force that is deployed as physical action toward $\vec{d}$ -fulfillment. And, as $\vec{d}$ -fulfillment is invariably linked to outcomes pertaining to the ever-changing outer world, the $\vec{d}$ -fulfillment matrix keeps altering as an ever-shifting goal post. As a result, success or failure could never get a reference plane, which remains stable against the ever-renewing configuration of the goal or the idea of success. The $\vec{d}$ -fulfillment process could, therefore, remain incessantly active in mind, consuming a man's physical, mental, and psychological energies, all at one time.

Now, let us consider a scenario where the mind is aligned with intellect, which in turn has a strong connect with integrative and undifferentiated consciousness and its time-tested pool of memories. The otherwise discriminating intellect could, in this scenario, behoove the undifferentiated consciousness and pass on integrative pulses to the mind and transform the individualistic goal into a unitive mission. The differentiated desires could then transform into integrated assent through reciprocal exchanges between mind and such an intellect. The desires then stabilize, and over a period of time, subside either through fulfillment or their willful negation—and at some stage, the mind could even get rid of these desires altogether. Instead of getting constantly engaged in object-focused, short-lived, and ever-changing pursuits, the mind could then function conforming to its design-purpose—to accurately receive and transmit inputs from the phenomenal world to the intellect through sensory organs—and just that! The systematic process of integration of mind with intellect and establishing the functionality of mind to its design intent is when human actions could be denominated as in complete harmony with the abundance principle of integrative consciousness. Such an integrated mind–intellect system, even while in the field of intense action, could yet be in state of perfect balance and constancy. The things and beings of the world remaining the same, such mind could accommodate the unitive dimension of humanity. The desire prompted, anxiety whipped, and individual-centered actions could no more be generated. This state of desireless action delivers the holistic and collective happiness in each of man's life moments. This is *human flourish*, as we describe borrowing the phrase from Michael Pirson's book, *Humanistic Management* (2017).

The collective human flourish is the desideratum of any human endeavor—within the carrying capacity of the bio-gaia system—Pirson argues, as he elaborates the blueprint of his model humanistic management theme—the postulation in which human flourish is heedfully and immanently entwined with *human dignity*—*self-respect* as against self-regard—and *human well-being*—the *common good* around which humans are affiliated and organized by the very cause of the evolutionary process itself. Pirson's *humanistic perspective* is meticulously calibrated to protection of human dignity that values freedom, love, care, responsibility, and character. Accordingly, the key reason for survival of humans is their rational nature and for which dignity and well-being in the frame of ethics and morality are crucial. The highest aspiration and unmitigated desire of human—he reckons—is to achieve an eco-balanced level of well-being and to flourish ultimately in dignity. As against, the dominant and contagious *economistic perspective* to which the modern prejudice is mulishly assigned, he argues—characterizes human beings as uncaring and restrictedly self-centered with singular focus on self-augmentation without self-accountability and in which only the self-interest and self-consumption provide the conclusive rationale for what is valuable.

In his book *Resonance: A Sociology of Our Relationship to the World* (2019), Hartmut Rosa, Professor of Sociology at the Friedrich-Shiller-Universität Jena, Germany, as well argues that the relational quality of man's relationship to the world is established by the fact that he (subject pole) desires something that appears attractive to him (world pole) or fears something that appears repulsive. Although, analytically, desire and fear constitute an opposition, both are completely intermixed, as desire as a palpable form of resonance comes up against the fear of being repulsed—argues Rosa. Therefore, without analyzing desire or fear (often the partial cause of desire) caused by attraction or repulsion (inverse-attraction), the fundamental driving force and existential mode of man's being or, his resonant bio-gaia relationship or, in Rosa's words, the *vibrating wire* connecting him with the world—that is, how he passively experiences and actively confronts what he desires and fears—cannot be understood. In essence, as Rosa contends, a man's *biographically specific* fears and desires—corralling by way of his experiences of intense alienation and resonance over time—serve him as *deserts of alienation* and *oases of resonance*, providing a kind of directional compass for him through his life. For, it is the fears and desires of man that alone open specific paths for him and determine his *horizon of expectations* in order that he finds his way back to those oases of resonance—his memories of specific happy and fulfilled moments in the past that make him feel *sustained* in the world. In this way, Rosa affirms, memories (of past) and expectation (from future) are intrinsically connected with the structure of a man's fears and desires, so that every biographical event in his life could be understood as a story of searching for an *oasis of resonance* and avoiding *deserts of alienation*. Human desire is simply a desire for resonance—postulates Rosa—in other words, therefore—a desire for resonating with collective consciousness, which is not an emotional state, but a mode of relation beyond the realm of mind and intellect—a state of being related to the collective human, entirely—and an active readjustment of individualistic desires to the collective human flourish.

Therefore, incipiently, desires activate intellect, and subsequently, the entire life process is set into motion. The unitive collective consciousness, though watchful and aware, is unbiased and uninvolved in everyday affairs of the man. This is the universal and infinite pool of energy common to all things and beings and based on accumulated individual desires the man draws a finite share from it for his limited lifetime—what he does with it, however, remains completely his own business! All the five planes of human existence and sustenance, therefore, coordinatively function within his being. The animative and breath planes combine is a man's gaia body. The mind and intellect planes together constitute a man's cognitive body. The consciousness plane is termed his causal body, simply because it causes the manifestation of cosmic energy into his individual being with a unique body–mind–intellect system characterized by a unique combination of kinetic and potential energies inherent in the cumulate of unfulfilled desires. In other words, gaia, cognitive, and causal body combine to shape the total human with unique individual consciousness within the abundance of universal collective consciousness.

The Attributes of Being: Human Personality Characteristics

The dynamics of $\bar{d}$-fulfillment not only cause the manifestation of a man's individual consciousness, but also profiles his sui generis personality attributes that determine the propensity and disposition of his actions in the phenomenal world. The three principal attributes of desire that profile the unique personality of a man are:

1. Dynamic equilibrium (DE)
2. Stimulated entropy (SE)
3. Chaotic inertia (CI)

The DE energy in desire is dynamic in the nature of constancy of abundance-spirited collective consciousness. The SE energy is also dynamic, but in the nature of accelerating and scarcity-driven individual consciousness. The CI energy, at the other end, is inert and in the nature of directionless and confused consciousness. In other words, this is the consciouslessness that is neither collective nor individual. In a man, all the three attributes are necessarily present, but in different allocations. This is the key to understand the differences in tendencies and proclivities among the individuals. In Vedic literatures, this is termed as guna (attributes) theory.

The higher the proportion of DE energy in a man, the stronger are his ethical propensities. Therefore, transcendence and collectiveness come naturally and easily to man when greater DE prevails in his desires. A preponderance of SE, while imparts strong action orientation to the man, his desires inevitably carry the attributes of scarcity—greed, anger, jealousy, vanity, cunning, vindictiveness, and so on. These constituent psychological forces of SE are the prime movers of his unethical leanings. The CI lacks action orientation, yet includes many of the negative psychological tendencies—the dis-values—of SE and thereby breeds in man a sort of passive, unproductive, and unethical disposition. The SE man wants to contest but win, while the CI man wants to win even without contesting. The DE man is the wisdom man who possesses an integrative knowledge that could see unity even in diversity. The SE man and CI man are intelligent men who apprehend all beings in multiplicity and mutual distinction without the appreciation of any underlying unity. It is important to note that the innate capacity of man to distinguish between what is ethical and what is not in different situations is not so much linked to his power of intellectual analysis as to the more basic psychological tendencies ($\overline{d}$-fulfillment) shaping his bio-gaia personality. The human personality attributes, therefore, influence the very character of his intellectual analysis and its outcome.

Being in Mind–Intellect Dynamics

With this background, we could now assuredly examine the functioning of mind in a man's everyday life. Essentially, the mind performs two distinct and foundational functions—objective and subjective. The objective mind or the emotional mind or simply the mind is outer world oriented that receives the stimuli from the objects of the world. The subjective mind or the intellect, however, is (man's) inner world oriented that reacts or responds to the stimuli received from the objective mind. Thus, mind comes under the causal influence of intellect. A balanced mind–intellect personality will necessarily have harmonious functioning between the mind and intellect. However, with epochal exceptions, the mind and intellect in human personality are functionally split and misaligned due to an intervening layer of unfulfilled desires, accumulated and hoarded by the man. The thicker this layer, greater would be the degree of misalignment between intellect and mind and weightier would be entropy of desires within a man's cognitive personality. *I want it,* is subterfuge for *cry!* See Figure 1.2.

At each moment as the man receives different sets of stimuli, intellect accumulates newer impressions of desires superimposed on unresolved impressions of the residual desires. Therefore, the action triggered by the intellect will carry the flavor of current as well as accumulated desires.

Desire is the primal cause of all human actions. It's the desire that
constructs the personal identity of a man and effectively separates
him from human. *I want it.* is the other name of *crv!*

Figure 1.2 Desire, mind, and intellect dynamics

The stimuli coming from the action episodes, as they incident upon the
mind, disturbs its entropy, and to resettle that, it relies on an intellect
that has rational and discretionary capabilities. Therefore, a strong link
and infallible alignment between mind and intellect is necessary. The
unsettled entropy is the potential source of creating new layers of unresolved desires over the intellect, and that could insulate mind even more
singly to a left-to-itself state. And, the mind then could only act sans
any input from intellect. As a consequence, the man gets detached from
his abundance consciousness, and his actions lose association with the
abounding abundance principle.

In other words, when the man works confined only to his bio-gaia
sense, he could just perceive the world of objects; when he works in
the dominion of mind, he could experience the world of emotions;
and when he works lead by intellect, he could comprehend the world
of ideas. The objective world is, therefore, perceived and experienced
never as such, but only as interpreted by a man's mind and intellect.
And, as man is not merely a body, but an integrated body–mind–intellect system with a desire pattern and unique attributes, his experiences
are different even for same objects at different times. Desire is what

ultimately determines a man's unique identity through the mind–intellect dynamics.

Mind and Intellect: Constrained in Scarcity

As a man's desires are focused on the objective world, his mission of life remains object focused and constrained in finites. And, his relationship with the phenomenal world remains limited to working out $\bar{d}$-fulfillment in the finite extents of his lifetime. The finitude of lifespan within the objective world is the genesis of scarcity mentality of the man, in which he is an ever-constrained actor, competing with all other fellow actors in the survival-of-the-fittest mode. Desires, instead of ideas, take the center stage, and mind, which is primarily appointed to transmute ideas into action, gets engaged in $\bar{d}$-fulfillment sans the ideas. Over a period of time, such a scarcity mind begins to corrupt the intellect itself and corrodes its conviction into dogmas in a sort of reverse osmosis phenomenon. Therefore, with every augmented gap between the mind and intellect, a man's actions keep losing the necessary direction and strength to mitigate his life challenges and fulfill his desires.

There is no doubt that mind alone triggers all human actions, and yet, the reverse is not only true but highly effectual. The physical pose and poise as well develop a corresponding attitude of the mind. So, while the mental mood determines human actions, the resultant physical attitude and conduct in turn induce a corresponding mood makeover in the mind. In a way, therefore, the mind influences action and outcomes of the action in turn influence mind, and the gap between mind and intellect keeps widening. Then, the actions triggered by this left-to-itself mind in such scenarios are largely the emotional outbursts or indiscriminate impulses. A constrained mind in scarcity is, therefore, erratic and unsteady.

Being and Destiny: The Cause–Effect Phenomenon

As we discussed, desires cause the beings and even nonbeings are just a supplementary manifestation of man's desires. It would, therefore, be pertinent to discuss the underpinning of the law of causation and touch upon Newton's *Mathematical Principles of Natural Philosophy* one more time in this context. In a nutshell, the Newtonian philosophy of the law of causation could be summated in a set of four simple rules:

1. There could be no effect without a cause.
2. The effect is cause itself in another form.
3. When cause is removed from effect, nothing remains in the effect.
4. The cause is simultaneous and intrinsic in the effect.

The play of cause and effect takes place only in the medium of time in which the cause is precedent in time and effect is subsequent. In other words, cause is past, and effect is present, and the present itself becomes cause with reference to the future. Thus, the present is not only an effect, but also the cause for the future. In philosophical terms, the effect of man's past action could be referred to as destiny, and his actions toward $\bar{d}$-fulfillment constitutes his free will. The man has, thus, a choice of how he could deal with his destiny in the domain of his free will. In other words, while man's present turns out as a fait accompli, he is indeed the architect of his future.

The future is, therefore, caused by man's actions, and the time domain of actions is always the present. Now, if the mind could get access to the intellect, it could draw upon its resources—the time-tested ideas and consolidated ideals. And several action options could be generated and evaluated by the intellect with reference to past memories saved within it. If the mind–intellect connect is partially or fully impaired due to accumulated unfulfilled desires, the actions triggered by the mind primarily bear the color of these desires. The basic nature and potency of action could, therefore, undergo change, and as a result, a yet wider gap is created between the mind and intellect. And this sequence perpetuates as "cause-the-action and effect-the-destiny" phenomenon through a man's lifetime.

Happiness: The Pursuit of Desire

Let us pick any of a man's action exploits, and ask the question, why is he doing what he is doing, and repeat the question one more time over the response to the previous *why*. And repeat this question routine 4 to 5 times. In the end, we are most likely to get just the one final response— "I want to be happy." That means, *to be happy* is really the axiomatic pursuit of man. Now, let us explore, what happiness is. And, as we are yet to experience the hitherto unexplored happiness, we would not know what this could be like. We must, therefore, execute our search from the other end, that is, what happiness is not, and for that, pick an object for the purpose of this enquiry. Now, if the happiness is inherent in the experimental object, then it should provide the same measure of happiness to different people at the same time and the same person at different times. Indubitably, this could not be true—therefore, happiness for man is not an objective, but entirely a subjective phenomenon having a distinct and clear relationship with his state of mind.

Efficiency of Free Will: The Key Differentiator

As a bio-gaia entity man too is governed by physical laws and, yet, in him, because of his subjective dimension, a certain measure of efficiency is set up through his free will to manage his actions in pursuits of happiness. This additional port of self-cultivated efficiency, we call the efficiency of free will, is arranged through the subjective personality of man, and puts him to an advantage over the other life forms in the gaia-system. The efficiency of free will is, therefore, to be seen as freedom in man to willfully set up his abilities and capabilities in the field of action. The efficiency of free will, thus, manages not just the limitations of a man, but also, as a distinguishing tool, helps him to explore and realize higher levels of subjective reality in a continuum to his abundance consciousness self.

Idea, Ideals, and Field of Action

There is, as such, an incessant ebb of cosmic energy flowing through the plane of breath in the human personality. The energy in the breath is dynamic and the propensity of its movement is to realize $\bar{d}$-fulfillment for the man. The degree of its dynamism is palpably linked to the quality of $\bar{d}$ in terms of its measure of collectiveness and the resultant ethical sanction it receives from the intellect. A goal set by way of careful evaluation by the intellect, comprising its ideas and ideals, is likely to be congruent with ethics–abundance principle and therefore valid for a longer timeframe. And, once the mind accepts this goal without any infractions from everyday desire impulses of shorter wavelength, an ethics-centric dynamism is set in motion within the mind–intellect system. Ethical dynamism acts as a countervailing force to the onslaught of negative energy, not aligned to the ethics principle, coming from the phenomenal world. Therefore, discovery of ideals within could be crucial to establishing man in the vitality of his infinite dimension, in his fullness, in his completeness, in the abundance.

Managing Energy: The Scarcity–Abundance Exchange

As a scarcity entity, man could draw only finite energy for a finite span of his lifetime. Therefore, it becomes important to understand how he could leverage this energy in support of his ideas and ideals to fulfill his desires and how diligently he manages this energy to pre-empt the unproductive intemperance's in everyday life. In the human personality system, dissipation of this psychological energy could occur only through three channels:

1. Past (fear) channel: Memories of the past tend to influence and direct human actions in line with outcomes in the past. As a consequence, the energy required for creative inputs to actions is reduced or even dry up. The final outcome is, therefore, a repeat of the past or lesser. A large portion of psychological energy is, thus, consumed to cope with the *fear of failure*.
2. Future (anxiety) channel: Anxieties pertain to the domain of future, which is vague until realized or created. Any energy directed to vagueness is likely to be ineffective and therefore inefficient. A large portion of a man's psychological energy is similarly consumed to deal with the *butterflies in stomach*.
3. Present (worry) channel: Excitement of the present fibs focus, therefore, dissipates energy. The already depleted stock of energy, as a result of its overallocation to the past and future, impacts the field judgment necessary to manage the action episodes in the

present. And, therefore, poor judgment, coupled with overexcitement to exploit speedier $\bar{d}$-fulfillment, impacts the execution of present endeavors and coupled with anxieties relating to future causes increased worries in the present like the *skating on thin ice*.

Prof. Vijay Govindarajan of Tuck School of Business in his book, *The Three-Box Solution* (2016), says, "...selectively forget the past, manage the present, and create the future, as a strategy for leading innovation." We subscribe to this and observe its validity even in domains beyond economics and business, as envisaged by the professor. All human actions, whatever be their nature, participate in an energy exchange process in conformity with physical laws. Even a misdirected activity develops a new pattern of energy form. Therefore, managing energy not only involves managing its quantitative, the objective dimension, but also involves managing its propensity, the qualitative, the subjective dimension. Even a highly energetic man could be quite ineffective if the energy flow within him is overly misdirected into past or overwhelmingly concentrated in the future. Only through an intelligent reorientation of mental attitudes, could man conserve his psychological energy and direct it to action episodes in the domain of present.

Let us now examine the subjective import of this principle. The past is what defines the self-image of a man, and his present actions are just the idea of enhancing his self-image to a new level in line with his $\bar{d}$-fulfillment. Desires within him essentially fuel all his actions. However, if desires are adequately evaluated by an intellect, fully alert, and aware in abundance consciousness with its large reservoir of memories, each of the desire elements could be transmuted into conviction, an altogether different energy pattern, which could be past and future proof. And, this way, therefore, the energy dissipation could largely be reduced or completely neutralized. While desires stimulate motivation, it is the conviction that in effect simulates inspiration. The depth of conviction, however, depends on the loftiness of the ideas and immutability of the ideal within. While desires rush toward the ordinated goal, conviction progresses toward a mission, a superordinate goal beyond any constricting coordinates in terms of the collectivity of its scope and omnitude of time. Conservation of energy could, therefore, be worked out by diligently subduing the entropy of thoughts within the scarcity mind. It is like engaging with the scarcity world outside, keeping a complete and firm connect with the abundance world inside.

Goal and Superordinate Goal

Man's action could only be as agreeable as the goal sanctioned by his ideals. Although an ideal is comprehension of intellect, it is the mind that *de facto* cognates a goal. If this goal is based on ideals, then man's vision is likely to extend beyond the coordinates of his individual self to the larger collective self, and the goal matures into a superordinate goal. The motivation of scarcity mind transmutes into inspiration of abundance mind with sharper focus and compliance to universal abundance principle. The superordinate goal carries the energy pattern of longer wavelength and, therefore, dissipates not impetuously through psychological holes created on the mental plane by fears of past, anxieties of future, or worries of present. All energy could, thus, be directed to fulfill such superordinate goal. This indeed is the synchronized functioning of body, mind, and intellect that could configure the best possible personality model for the man in a given time. This is the inspired mood of a man, which is likely to evince a happy response from deeper abundance consciousness much beyond his scarcity consciousness. Inspired work not only brings out higher efficiency in his actions, but distributes greater dividend for the man by virtue of collective human flourish thus delivered.

Re-educated Values and Readjusted Mind

The mind–intellect system is essentially an understanding tool that always tries to apprehend things in sympathy with the pattern of desires accumulated therein. In other words, it responds to the unique propensity of accumulated desires or the urges. As a result, man could interpret things only under the light of these urges, even if facts point otherwise and understanding of the facts may not reach the necessary depths of mind and thereby tends to paint the facts in patterns liken to his urges. The urges in a scarcity mind could simply be classified under three broad categories—the physical urges, the social urges, and the urge to know.

The urges, in unique combination of these three categories, combine to develop an urge pull that exists in a man's psychological body, just like gravitational pull that acts upon his bio-gaia physical body. In a way, the urge pull holds the man in the midst of all things and happenings in the world. At any moment, as part of larger human body, man is generally engaged in a standard way of doing things, which in other words could simply be termed as imitating the world as it is—and because we live as we are living, we are as we are. Therefore, to propel life into a higher plane of existence, the man would necessarily need to modify and alter his urges.

However, through re-education and readjustment of scarcity mind, when the urge pull is aligned to the abundance principle, man is evolved. This readjustment is not to subdue the individuality of the man, but to enable him to perform on a higher plane of abundance consciousness with a wider and deeper vision of the affairs of the world. To withdraw the mind engaged in goal-seeking pursuits and readjust it to the inspiring contemplation of the superordinate goal while at the same time, giving the mind the fertile ground to function with ennobling ideals is, what we call, re-educating the mind to the collective abundance principle.

Unreal Scarcity and Real Abundance

Life in the envelopments of matter is finite in as much as that every little experience at all three levels of existence—among the objects, with the emotions, and in the ideas—is finite. The body changes in every moment—mind evolves, and intellect grows the same way. All changes, evolutionary movements, and growth are indicated by a constant cessation of their previous state, in order that the things concerned may change, evolve, and grow. In other words, it is clearly established that the body, mind, and intellect are ever changing, and all of them have finite existence. Moreover, specific objects of the world, including the human body, have a touch-and-feel reality within their respective finitude. We could, therefore, say that the specific world object, including the human body, is real as well as finite. We are, therefore, affront with finite though, but a real world!

However, with no such touch-and-feel kind of reality, mind and intellect are just psychological bodies, albeit within a finite existential framework. We could call them unreal finite or unreal scarcity. Furthermore, for change to take place and perceived, a changeless vein is necessary. Therefore, in order to hold together life experiences at three levels—body, mind, and intellect—and to construct an experience of the integrated whole—we call life—it is explicable to have a changeless lamina, the real vein. This real is the abundance consciousness, the discerning awareness. Abundance consciousness remains the same, no matter the experience of man in his life time. It is, therefore, the real invariable—it is the real abundance. Problem of scarcity, thus, cannot be solved unless abundance has replaced it—paucity is not excised unless plenty has replaced it—and weakness in man is not cured unless he is re-established in strength. Scarcity experience within and through the body, mind, and intellect can be mastered only if the man could discover and establish an identity with the abundance of the collective consciousness, the real abundance.

Self-Actualization to Self-Realization

Self-realization is not an end-state experience of human; rather, it is the culmination of a life lived collectedly and made progressively more free from any entanglements with the lower-order gross existence, freedom from discrete outcomes, and the finite outlook. It is the all-inclusive transformation of man to be perfected by way of *stilling the mind* through abundance-centered creed inertia that is tuned to collective human needs. It is the ascension from scarcity to abundance—taking the ethics–abundance strides to go beyond the individualistic personal happiness's to the collective human flourish. Self-realization is not a sudden superimposition of a special knowledge, but the culmination of an evolutionary process in a man's life.

All activities that man undertakes in his lifetime are due to a desire to obtain a greater amount of happiness or, in other words, to achieve greater freedom from unhappiness. This is the idea of a better life as the man visualizes. However, a better life is sustainable only when singular individual happiness turns into collective human flourish. Real progress is when he evolves from an individual self to a collective self. All the so-called milestones in the history of human progress are nothing but man's victory over a source of unhappiness and overcoming the limitation imposed on him by the world at large. It is a struggle to replace unhappiness with happiness. The flight of man from discomfort to comfort is what he considers as progressing to higher standard of living. However, it is utopian to rearrange an ever-changing pattern of life to a specific configuration in perpetuity. Therefore, despite the best efforts in planning, organizing, leading, and controlling (P-O-L-C) by the "man" in "manager," his life remains riddled with sequent of disappointments.

In the happiness continuum, any point below the next higher is unhappiness, and therefore, the pursuit for happiness is the pursuit of *more* at ever-accelerating greed–speed to get the better of scarcity, no matter the standard of living man has already reached. Although man could arrive at the highest possible stratum of his psychological existence, averred to as self-actualization in Maslow's need hierarchy, he is never off-ramp the slippery slopes of so-called progress—any drop in speed of action plummets him back to yet lower level of individuality. It is, therefore, clear that while bio-eye could accurately see the finite and real world, the eye of mind, or the scarcity eye, could only see a desperately limited and inverted image of it, which is finite though, but projects just the unreal scarcity. And, mind, being the driver-in-chief, steps on to an excessively accelerated greed–speed action to combat the projected scarcity up the slippery slopes of progress in order to secure an abode in self-actualization. The need hierarchy, thus, turns into a greed hierarchy.

The only possible remedy to exit unreal scarcity is to connect back to the infinite abundance consciousness and realize real abundance in the authority of ever-witnessing abundance eye. This alone could reel back the image of unreal scarcity created by the mind to one of infinite real abundance—the very cause of the finite and real world. Greed hierarchy is then transposed into creed hierarchy, with two additional levels of existence added to the five levels—I exist, I desire, I control, I love, I express—postulated in Maslow's need hierarchy. The added levels, as we find, are: "I witness," therefore, I am wholly aware, and "I am," the abundance consciousness itself. And, the race up the slippery slopes transmutes into moral strides in a step to self-realization. It is, therefore, paradoxical

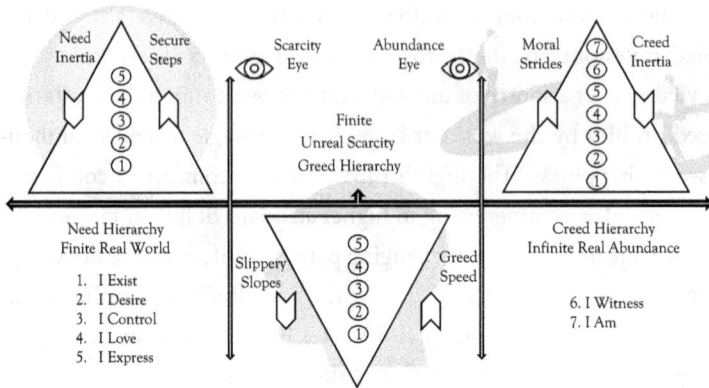

Figure 1.3 Self-actualization to self-realization

that mind could discern reality not when it is focused on the outer objective world, but apprehends truth only when it contemplates on the inner subjective world. It is only when the mind turns away from scarcity consciousness into the realm of abundance consciousness, it could comprehend the man in human, see Figure 1.3.

Back to Managing the Manager

There are two ways to approach day-to-day living—one is with the fact that man is a finite entity with a clear beginning and a clear end. The other is in the truth that man is part of the infinite expressed through several finite entities in congruence with universal abundance principle. The animative body—the equipment of expression for man—remains true to the laws of phenomenal world. However, the psychological body, comprising mind and intellect, is not constrained by the animative laws of existence and could therefore align readily with the abundance principle. The acclimation of man's psychological body in the abundance consciousness is expressed in three different ways at three different levels of his personality:

1. At an animative personality level, man is an individual personality governed by physical laws of the objective outer world as well as ethical laws of subjective inner world. In other words, he manages and, at the same time, he needs to be managed.
2. At the psychological personality level of the mind–intellect domain, he is part of collective personality; therefore, he is self-managed.

Figure 1.4 Managing the manager

3. At the personality plane of collective consciousness however, he is the collective personality itself and the owner of his own self.

In other words, the relationship of abundance-centric man with the phenomenal world is organized along the scarcity–abundance continuum. Moreover, the three personality attributes are not in conflict with each other, as they, rather, constitute the personality continuum of man to realize his primordial existence in abundance. As man progresses along this personality continuum, the owner and owned merge into one, and he enjoys greater degree of freedom in the flourish of a collective human, see Figure 1.4.

The Key Takeaway

1. Man can experience the objects of phenomenal world only through his five senses—the organs of perception. In search of happiness, man tends to gratify his senses in all possible ways. This is individual-centric living.

2. The uncaused cosmic energy or the life force is what we call the abundance consciousness. It pervades through all objects,

including human body, and allows man to express his individual self along the propensity of his unfulfilled desires amassed
in the memories of his intellect. These unfulfilled desires, we call
$\bar{d}$-fulfillment, determine and shape the individuality of man in
exclusive ways to react or respond uniquely to different stimuli.

3. Man wants happiness; therefore, there is a desire in him at all times in
   some form or other. Desire is the motivating force behind each of his
   actions (body), emotions (mind), and thoughts (intellect).

4. In order to experience happiness, the body, mind, and intellect must
   be in harmony with the objects, emotions, and thoughts. The mind
   and intellect function in the domain of ever-changing time. Therefore, happiness could only be short-lived as both the mind and intellect remain unstable all the time in the ever-changing times.

5. There is no common method applicable to the whole of mankind to
   be happy, simply as they are differently established in exclusive desire
   patterns. Therefore, based on the unique propensity of his urges that
   shape his personality mold, man could espouse any of the following
   approaches to sidestep the deep-seated scarcity in his cognitive personality and explore abundance beyond to re-establish his connect
   with the abundance consciousness:
   a. Intellectual personality type—approach through knowledge
   b. Emotional personality type—approach through dedication
   c. Balanced (fairly leveraged mind–intellect) personality type—
      approach through action
   d. Latent (unleveraged mind–intellect) personality type—approach
      through discipline
      There could, of course, be a blended approach as well to suit the
      unique personality combination man could possess or develop at
      different times in his lifetime.

6. The way to self-actualization is through the slippery slopes of greed
   hierarchy. It is, therefore, a relentless trial for the manager to manage
   both herself and the others. A possible recourse is to train the mind
   to transcend the unreal scarcity and assimilate the real abundance
   within to first manage the self.

CHAPTER 2

Abundance: The Ethics Paradigm

The Abundance Principle

Science is essentially an order of structured thinking with a spirit of petition into the objective–outer world. But there is another equally important subjective–inner world that still remains to be investigated. For that, an order of thinking in the spirit of rumination is called for. This essentially is the investigation of the subject by the subject itself, who regularly interacts even with the objects as well. In other words, the petitioner himself or herself needs to be investigated. This unique investigation is, what we call, rumination. The object that the scientist observes and tries to comprehend could be completely vague for him or her if she—the observer—is absent. Therefore, in any given experience, the experiencer—the subject—is the counterpart to the experienced—the object.

In other words, man, the experiencer is the subject who gains experience of the outer world through his own instruments of experience—his body and mind–intellect system. All experiences that man stacks up in his lifetime are either through his body or mind or the intellect. Therefore, man the subject, is neither the body nor mind and not intellect, as they are merely his instruments of experience, although he maintains a very intimate relationship with each one of them. As a matter of scheme, an observer is necessarily different from any instrument of observation and the object observed. We could, therefore, say that man is not his body when he experiences objects, not his mind when he experiences feelings and, not his intellect when he ruminates on ideas. The principle that underpins all that the intellect thinks, mind feels, and body perceives is life principle, we call, the abundance principle or the ethics–abundance principle of collective consciousness. This is akin to electrical energy flowing through discrete equipment, but all expressing it differently in accordance with their respective designs and configuration. Ethics–abundance principle sets the process of evolution in motion and sustains it incessantly in a perpetual cycle of time. It promises no magical vicissitudes in the phenomenal world, but it enables man to psychologically reorient himself in poise and balance in everyday moments through his lifetime.

The objective world subsists, functions, and plays its follies according to the temporal dominion and phenomenal laws over which man has absolutely no control—just as he has no control over laws of gravitation. Objects in this world engage with a man's mind to simulate an experience for him. Therefore, if mind could be acculturized to respond only within the awareness of abundance principle, then such response is likely to be abundance-like—collective, unitive, unfragmented, and balanced in perpetual constancy. With such an abundance-centric mind, intellect could see the congruence in discrete, and mind could feel the happiness even without any specific self-attachment. The scarcity mind, as we discussed, could fancy only the incomplete and disjointed experience limited to the individual self, while the abundance mind could experience the same phenomenal world totally in its ubiquitous dignity. The scarcity mind is nothing, but a pile of differentiated memories of a finite and scarcity-afflicted world nurtured by man as individual-centric desires to be fulfilled in some future time. In other words, the scarcity mind configures its past-based and future-focused memory personality, which has evidently no relevance in the present. More the man pivots in abundance, more his "memory personality" becomes dormant. A present-focused mind, therefore, must be completely aligned with intellect, which must correspond with the ethics–abundance principle.

Ethics and Abundance Entwine

As history of scientific progress has shown, its knowledge is always instrument conditioned, whether these instruments are our unaided senses or the more refined gadgets and devices or even subtler cyber routines and programs. Moreover, this knowledge is dependent upon interpretation extricated from a set of observed data, and, at the same time, dependent on the observer who is observing the data. For instance, a human body could mean a collection of bones and tissues or a collection of cells or giant molecules or even protons, electrons, and neutrons or simply pure condensed energy to different investigators. That is to say, a solid-looking human body could mean differently to different observers or investigators. While investigators could be interpreting the fact from their own specific point of view, none could claim a greater reality than the other, as each one is conditioned by a specific level of investigation and the instruments they deploy.

However, mind, as we know, is an instrument with a flowing stream of thoughts. We also know that the goal-seeking desire ($\overline{d}$-fulfillment) is the primary source for generating such thoughts. Therefore, if by some means, we could eliminate desires and pause the thoughts, we could arrive at direct knowledge that is mind-free, instrument-free or, in other words, nonmediate. This direct knowledge that we retrieve is un-interpreted and undistorted by any medium and, therefore, could take us closer to reality and truth. This direct knowledge is not empirical and therefore stands on its own in the truth of universal collective consciousness. In other words, this is the knowledge of abundance consciousness, the knowledge of infinite abundance. And, it transcends all the faculties of knowledge or the instruments of measurement and establishes a direct contact with reality that is the abundance consciousness. Therefore, the knowledge of abundance is retained all by itself in the abiding ethics–abundance principle that maintains and sustains the entire cosmic ethics–abundance system.

The abundance consciousness is uncaused in the supposition implied in our arguments. However, only the caused phenomenon could be seen or perceived as manifested and existent, not the eventuation uncaused. Therefore, abundance consciousness could be perceived only through a process of negation of all that were manifested and perceived. Adi Shankaracharya, the early 8th century Vedic philosopher and seer-scientist, suggested a systematic process of negation in his poetic composition in Sanskrit called *Nirvana Shatikam* to realize the uncaused consciousness, self-sustained in the abiding ethics–abundance principle. It could, therefore, be concluded that the existence and non-existence of a being is simultaneous and contingent upon its cause–effect relationship with the abundance consciousness. Something could be experienced as existing or not existing only when we are conscious of its existence and simultaneously of its nonexistence. In a cause–effect relationship, the cause is converted into effect only when there is a material cause, an equipment cause, and an efficient cause—all combining together in the will of man, the dynamic entity, who lends this will through his intelligence to make it function commensurate to the will.

The abundance principle manifests through two principal forces: power to act and power to know, applied sequentially. First the power to act, when applied, rides on our mind through sense organs to the objects and molds the psycho constitution or the desires in the mind into form of the object. Then, the power to know illumines the form into an experience of— I know it, it is there, and I am aware. If the mind is individual-centric or as we call scarcity-centric, only the individual experience is manifested, and if the mind is collective- or abundance-centric, a collective experience consistent with the universal ethics–abundance principle is manifested.

Humanizing the Mind: The Relational Framework

Mind, as we know, is a mere flow of thoughts. Quantity of thoughts flowing within the mind depends on the type of desires that create and maintain the essential nature of thoughts within the mind. The quality of thoughts is linked to degree of association of desires with the abundance principle. The direction of thoughts is linked to the memories from past, worries for future, and anxieties pertaining to changes taking place in the present. Therefore, humanizing the mind to abundance consciousness constitutes a composite scheme to change the quantity, quality, as well as the direction of flow of thoughts within the mind to bring about transformational change in composition and structure of human personality.

Moreover, the three components: quantity, quality, and direction, of the scheme are not mutually exclusive, but complementary to each other, and together, they provide a framework for humanizing the scarcity mind and link it to abundance consciousness. In this framework, man strives to understand through knowledge, act through action, and fulfill through

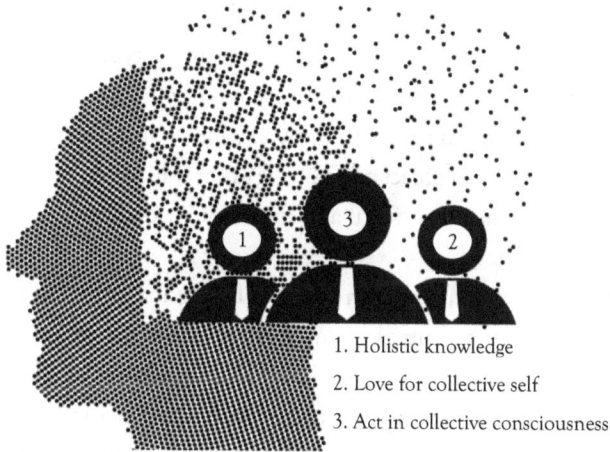

1. Holistic knowledge
2. Love for collective self
3. Act in collective consciousness

Figure 2.1 The humanizing framework

love, the collective abundance agenda and establish a relationship with the abundance consciousness. A man in abundance mind, desires individual self-ness and independence simultaneously with collective self-ness and interdependent affiliation with fellow humans. It is, therefore, a relationship framework linking man in scarcity with human in abundance in pursuance of knowledge or action or love or any unique combination corresponding man's subjective personality, see Figure 2.1.

The Scarcity Mind: Evaluator and Maximizer

In a scarcity scenario, man tries to evaluate and optimize his desire fulfillments within a given set of constraints arranged within a set of hedged boundary conditions. He bids different trade-offs and substitutes, albeit within the finite perimeters. Being finite, more of one lessens the rest of others. Therefore, his evaluation process eventually leads to judging the situation to pick one but drop the other. And, while *pick* is to fulfill the desire—therefore a success—*drop*, leaves within his mind, a feeling of unfulfillment—therefore a failure—even if it was meant quite naturally to be so in the scheme of things designed by the man himself. Therefore, to-be judgmental is never a prudent way of being for the man simply because failure remains embedded in success at all times and in all situations. Moreover, in all such evaluation exercises, some objective value is invariably to be assigned to the options and outcomes under evaluation, which is impractical and error prone in most of everyday life situations. The root desire of man, as we discussed, is to be happy, which in turn is linked to what he values subjectively and not objectively. The flow of value is from subject to object and not the other way round. The objective value, by itself, remains notional and therefore incapable of fulfilling the root desire of man.

In the scarcity scenario, man tends to be the maximizer too because his unlimited wants are pitted against limited opportunities in the space-time domain. He is, therefore, constrained at all times, as life episodes appear to him the stumbling blocks that he must overcome to fulfill his desires. He is also constrained by the limits of his own knowledge about various opportunities and choice of actions to meet his goals and tends to reconcile with the *good enough*, rather than the best that he hopes for. Therefore, maximization eventually leads to diminished self-esteem and curtailed satisfaction from episodes of life. Thus all human creativity gets directed and employed only to fulfill unfulfilled desires.

The Abundance Mind: Collaborative and Cooperative

Owing to finitude of things and beings, a methodological individualism is bound to set the basis for man's everyday living. As its unintended consequence, man as individual self is seen as an isolationist needing no embedded-ness and driven by exchangeability for fulfillment of his desires. However, on the abundance plane, he is un-individual—not divisible. In the sense of abundance, he could, therefore, restore the psychological inter-connectedness back in mind for his inter-dependent existence in life. Interdependence, and therefore collaboration, is an existential principal in conformity with the abundance principle. One of the main features of human psyche is collaboration, and it is, so to say, hardwired in human personality, and consequently, group forming is a fundamental human trait and a decision-making tool. In the wake of collaborative impulses, man develops emotions that drive him to ethical bonding and behave and act in the sense of abundance for cooperative outcomes to the benefit of collective human. Such collaboration is, thus, an element of the ethics–abundance principle and not mere aphorism. It is our natural social instinct that leads man to take pleasure in the company of others and feel a certain amount of sympathy with them and even perform some services for them. We shall discuss collaboration more elaboratively in the context of competition in the following pages.

Realigning Individual-Self to Collective-Self

Being the existential consciousness, the ethics–abundance principle is implicit in the collective sense of man. It differs from cooperation, as the collective sense requires no direct reciprocity, and no mutual exchange is imminent in it, as the individual self is subsumed in collective self itself. Man is called a social animal not without reason, as it underpins an existential meaning into it and channelizes his collective desire into action for manifestation of his collective existence. However, even as collectiveness is the natural being of man, a special role of individualism and individual uniqueness is seen more pronounced in man's everyday thoughts and actions due to his survive-first instincts. Hence, realignment of individual self with the collective self could be the key to develop a framework of universal code that can help build bridges between men pursuing diverse ideas, thoughts, and actions.

The foundation of ethics is, therefore, indwelling in the perpetuality of abundance. The ethics–abundance principle of collective existence is a non-negotiable standard that sets the ethics–abundance framework of norms and maxims to upraise and upheld human dignity itself. Hence, the synchronization of man's everyday routines and protocols with the ethics–abundance principle is omni-relevant—what applies to one applies to others as well, of course with some extrinsic and space–time based adjustments.

Dignity, Destiny, and Free Will

In keeping with the cause–effect principle, individual-centric desires $(\overline{d})$ cause the undivided abundance consciousness to manifest into divided scarcity consciousness of man. In other words, man is what his past $\overline{d}$-fulfillment actions were. If all his past actions were aligned to the ethics–abundance principle, then, in the present, he could hold his primordial dignity, the self-sustaining characteristic of the undivided human. In this way, the dignity and destiny of man is linked closely to his actions in the course of his everyday life. And, in this sense, we could inscribe the ethics–abundance principle as the *destiny principle* as well. Life of man is, thus, not just fate accompli, but a process, that he could self-control through his endowment of self-effort. Intellectual choice and direction of man's self-effort could change course of his destiny. The "present" destiny is of course caused by his past actions, but he could, by way of destiny principle, craft a future in personal dignity through self-effort and ethical choice of action. The future is, therefore, a continuity of the past modified in the domain of present. Freedom to modify the past and to create future for better or worse is self-effort or free will. In other words, what we meet in life is destiny, and how we meet destiny is free will.

Ethics–Abundance Paradigm: The Forethought

Scarcity, as we discussed, is a mind phenomenon and therefore unreal. Attempting to manage the real-world affairs with an idea that is unreal is not only unrealistic, but also unrealizable. The world, though finite, is real and must be probed with an even deeper and profound reality, the reality of the infinite abundance of collective consciousness within the human. And, for this, we need to sidestep the scarcity mind and consign its command and control functionality to the abiding ethics–abundance principle. It is with this background that we could deploy the insights from ethics–abundance principle itself to develop a system dynamics model to understand how man could engage with his sempiternal abundance that is shrouded with ostensible scarcity of his mind's make-believe world. And, for this, we need to retreat and recoup to the very same plane of collective consciousness and self-sustained abundance and examine the very marrow of desires that causes the expression of idea called man and drives the perpetuity of phenomenon called life. As we know, desires drive both the subjective and objective personality of man in sequential order—that means, first they drive the subjective self and then the subjective self drives the objective self of the man. It works like the *ratchet and pawl* mechanism that we find in applied mechanics.

The subjective ratchet supports and steps up the objective pawl of man's integrated subjective–objective personality to restore his primordial dignity and sanctions his action choices through his lifetime. In other words, the subjective–objective personality dynamics works in tandem to hold man's life in balance through action episodes in everyday life.

Ethics–Abundance: The Key Postulate

Before we proceed further to maturate our proposed ethics–abundance paradigm, it is importunate to posit the abundance principle in a precise system dynamics frame of reference, catching the constrained man in scarcity at the alpha point and visualizing the free human in abundance at the apogee. By now, we are also unhesitating to figure out that both of man's personality frames—scarcity self and abundance self—are equally hostile to any form of imposed collectivism. And both—self-managed individual self and self-sustained collective self—strive for dignity albeit in different ways. Similarly, both these dispositions emphasize human capacity for reasoning. In other words, therefore, freedom sets the empyrean measure of pristine human dignity.

In abundance, humans exteriorize their freedom through ethical–righteous social exchanges. And, such men engage with fellow humans, while at the same time, hedge and reinforce their respective humanity or dignity indoctrinated in the universal ethics–abundance principle. They treat each other as means, but also as end in themselves. This is not an ideal altruist stance, but the reason humans are human beings. Ethical behavior allows humans to build superior and longer-lasting relationships that enhance mutual trust and well-being. They are inspired to self-realize their being and serve others from the perspective of collective coexistence. Humans do not predictably follow maximization strategies, nor do they have fixed, preconceived utility functions in their action modules, but their interests, needs, and wants take shape through exposition and a program of continuous exchange in the phenomenal world. To bloom and blossom, such men, as the fundamental bio-gaia entity, balance their interests in consonance with the universal ethics–abundance principle, and align them with the sustainability of the planet and its ecological community, including fellow humans, animals, birds, flora-fauna, and all its reserves and resource. In abundance, therefore, being-ness in dignity is the foundational inspiration, and achieving balance between subjective–objective affirmation through action episodes in the course of lifetime is man's fundamental aspiration. Humans operate in ethical routines, yet learn and adapt constantly. The consummate vocation for man with the ethics–abundance perspective is to achieve an intransigent level of universal prosperity and human flourish.

The Baseline Model

In a nutshell, we could, therefore, propound that the unitive determination emerging from collective consciousness and self-serving desires emanating from individual consciousness drive every human action in sequence through two subjective motors that propel his determination. Two objective motors lunge his desires into motion. And, based on their unique determination and desire-based functionalities, the drive motor system could be modeled as comprising four distinct motors: two subjective and two objective motors.

Subjective motors drive the man to stabilize himself in present times, keeping appropriate balance between his past experiences and future aspirations and redeem his freedom, or we could say, inspire him to explore his evolution through involution. We call them the balancing (PPF—present, past, future) motor and the freedom (IEE—involution, explore, evolution) motor. Objective motors drive the man to accumulate, compete, and elate in the phenomenal world in order to secure his identity as individual and enable him to bond with things and beings of the world fostering his basic survival proclivity to effectively communicate, relate, and reflate. We call them the economic (ACE—accumulate, compete, elate) motor and the empathy (CRR—communicate, relate, reflate) motor. The economic motor is, therefore, a utility maximization motor that is complimentary to empathy motor, in the sense that the desire to be an individual self is incomplete without the desire to bond with other-selves and his desires pertaining to his physical, emotional, and intellectual urge ought to be fulfilled for him to be happy in the phenomenal world. It is, therefore, important to examine the role and interdependence of the subjective (PPF and IEE) motors and the objective (ACE and CRR) motors to decipher human roots in abundance consciousness and the construct

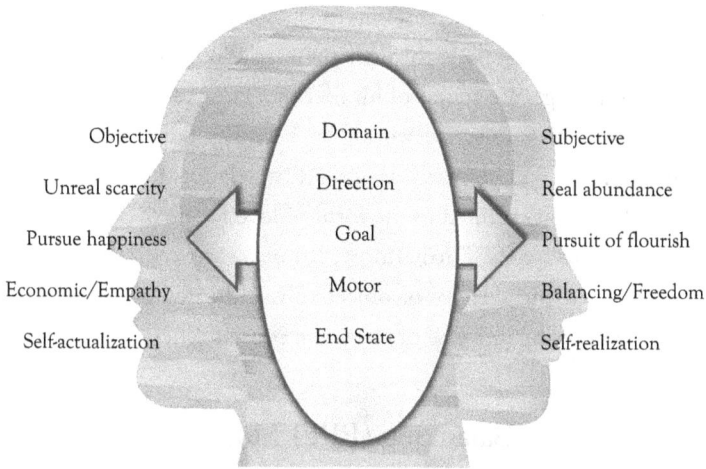

Objective	Domain	Subjective
Unreal scarcity	Direction	Real abundance
Pursue happiness	Goal	Pursuit of flourish
Economic/Empathy	Motor	Balancing/Freedom
Self-actualization	End State	Self-realization

Figure 2.2 The ethics–abundance paradigm

of humanity along the ethics–abundance principle to self-realize his existence in collective human flourish beyond self-actualization into plenary and self-absorbed happiness, see Figure 2.2.

Economic (ACE) Motor

Economic motor drives the economic agenda of man for his survival in the phenomenal world. To this end, he competes with others, earns his everyday living, and accumulates wealth and resources to manage his present time and the contingent future time. Man also strives to gain ever-higher grounds to elate himself and thereby secure a place in the immutability of self-actualization. However, when the very same man turns inward toward the subjective world, accumulation of wealth is recouped with accumulation of values, competing with other-selves is replaced with competing with individual self and the urge for self-actualization mutates to an implore for self-realization.

Empathy (CRR) Motor

Empathy motor drives the most basic desire of man to communicate and express his individual self through words and deeds in relation to other-selves in a *my own frame* of the world. And, toward this end, he formalizes relationships such as marriage, partnerships, and work-groups, within the prevailing temporal set up to ensure that his gains are safe and secure on an everyday basis through these relationships and his desires are fulfilled through the course of his lifetime. Here too, when man turns inward toward his subjective world, he becomes reflective and begins to communicate with himself as well. His relationships become self-established and self-retained in the form of love for its own sake and not for any reciprocal gains. Furthermore, his deeds get redirected to establish him, not in the scarcity of objective world, but the abundance of subjective world, the universe of collective consciousness.

Balancing (PPF) Motor

Balancing motor is the reverse of empathy motor. As we discussed, once man turns inward and operates through his subjective personality, all his deeds and actions get directed to establish his collective self over a recurrent past–present–future continuum. In other words, his actions— physical, emotional, or intellectual—continually perquisition a universal yardstick to justify and establish his worth in the context of his existence and progress in an ethical world order. He derives meaning to his actions through these connotations, regardless of any ensuing advantage that could accrue in terms of fulfilling his desires, providing contingencies to his future plans, or establishing bond in his relationships. The man, rather than doing things by way of instincts, tends to figure out things that could be meaningful in the collective sense of his being and without any desire or design for contingency or any unique relational need. For him, the past in this sense is a reservoir of time-tested ideas to hone his being to navigate with dignity through present times, and the superordinate goal in future is to realize his identity in self-fulfilled abundance where desire fulfillment is no more exigent.

Freedom (IEE) Motor

Likewise, the freedom motor is the reverse of economic motor. The objective metric gets altered to the subjective metric. Man looks for intrinsic value idolize, instead of extrinsic value credit, engages in collaboration instead of embroiling in competition—and instead of stimulating self-actualization, simulates self-realization of absolute freedom in the abundance of his subjective reality. He goes all out to explore his being, hitherto limited in the finitude of the objective world, in the realm of unlimited subjective world. He is now comfortable with unknown, untried, and untested, and his mind engages with the phenomenal world with detached attachment wherein the observed is separated from the observer, deeds are distanced from the doer, and experience is muted to the experiencer.

Enrooting the Interdependent Personality

Independence of balancing motor and freedom motor is the key to understanding human evolutionary psychology. Man with his unique mind–intellect structure could continually habituate in the somatic environment of present times, rather than relying on its adaption to the totemic environment of past times. The independent status of objective or the desire motors could mean satiation of ACE and CRR desires could occur without the satiation of PPF and IEE determination in the space of a finite lifetime. Man with a disciplined and still mind could reorient his focus from the objective domain to the subjective domain of his being. The very same individual self agenda could then reconfigure into a broad-based collective self program. Therefore, by reversing the polarity, the very same objective motors could as well be launched into as subjective motors. In other words, once desire motors are synchronized with an interdependent and complimentary dimension of human personality, the desire fulfillment process becomes harmonious rhythmic and rooted in the abundance of infinite collective consciousness along the ethics–abundance principle, see Figure 2.3.

The Key Takeaway

Ethics–abundance is the evolutionary personality dimension of man and the mandate of his collective consciousness. Human in individual identity is man with a unique set of unfulfilled and individualistic desires. *Managing desires* becomes synecdoche to *managing the man* himself. Dynamics of these desires are manipulated through four distinct desire

Empathy Motor   Freedom Motor

Communicate   *Accumulate values*
Reciprocal relationship   *Compete self*
Scarcity   *Self-realization*

O B J E T I V E   S U B J E T I V E   • • Infinity

Accumulate wealth   Reflect
Compete others   Singular relationship
Self-actualization   Abundance

Economic Motor   Balancing Motor

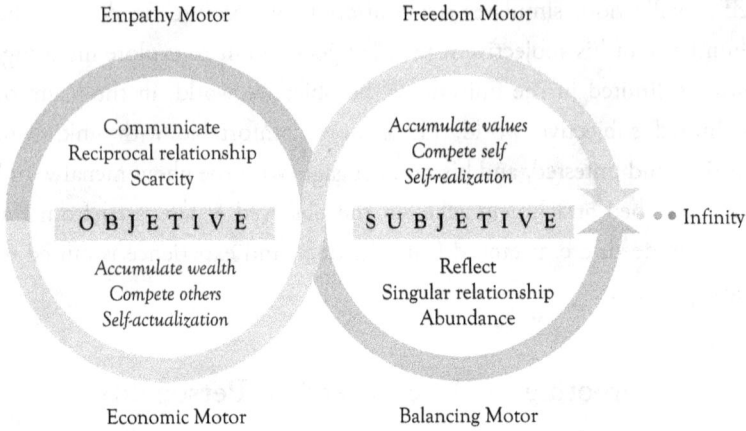

Figure 2.3 The abundance loop

motors, hardwired within the objective and subjective personality elements of the man. There are two objective motors—economic (ACE)
motor to drive his economic agenda and empathy (CRR) motor to fulfill
his emotional agenda—that all humans share. In addition, there are the
two subjective motors unique to man alone for him to realize the human
within. Subjective motors are the balancing (PPF) motor to synchronize
and align his existence along the past–present–future continuum in the
abundance consciousness and the freedom (IEE) motor that leads and
guides him to rediscover and realize his pristine glory and primordial dignity through self-realization. As desires are managed through a coordi-
nated performance of these four motors, man is set free from scarcity self
to his abundance self and matures into self-managed human along the
abiding ethics–abundance principle.

CHAPTER 3

Speed Versus Constancy: The Scarcity and Abundance Interplay

Including the human bio-gaia body, everything in nature in its undisturbed left-to-itself state, is rhythmic, unified, continuous, and steady. The only intrusive exceptions that we experience from time to time are brought about by invasive disruptions and interventions by the non-natural forces or phenomena. Continuity is, therefore, a natural process, and constancy is an intrinsic attribute of nature without any external-to-nature reference point. In humans, we could see these attributes in the bio-gaia rhythm of our body and the abundance consciousness of mind. Life processes, as we see, are evolutionary, and not revolutionary. The idea of speed and its inherent dynamic character seen in man is, therefore, linked to scarcity, the figment of his imagination, and not to real or any natural phenomenon. In other words, speed–constancy is an interplay of human existence in scarcity and abundance self. Therefore, the idea of speed is central to understanding the ethics dimension of man's sojourn in the phenomenal world.

Hartmut Rosa's Fisherman and Businessman

There is this fisherman, the hero in the story of *a fisherman and a businessman* that Hartmut Rosa recounts in his book, *Social Acceleration* (2015). The businessman tries to convince the fisherman who is sitting on the seaside beach fishing with a conventional fishing rod, to give up his inefficient method of fishing and instead adopt some modern methods to convert his routine of *just enough to earn a living* into a prospectively thriving fishing business that could engage scores of employees working for him possibly from all around the globe! Through a chain of rationalistic arguments, he tries to convince the fisherman to give up his archaic and conventional fishing method and instead leverage modern-day technology to earn enormous wealth for himself. And, moving along the design he suggests that the fisherman could deploy whopping material resources so amassed to contemplate a global fishing business. At the end of it, he could relax completely on the beach and enjoy his everyday time like never before. But, to the astonishment of the businessman, the fisherman dismissed all his argument saying he was already enjoying his time, and there was nothing new he could get from the set of complex activities suggested by the businessman! Let us, therefore, examine the ostensibly cogent design of the businessman and the businessman–fisherman confabulation little more closely.

In the narrative of progress enunciated by the businessman, even after a series of one-therefore-other sequence of activities, the end state of *relax on the beach,* is eventually identical to the state in the beginning when such activities were yet to be initiated. Even in the best-case scenario, the fisherman gets nothing different than what he already has. The model of progress outlined by the businessman seems trapped in an activity syndrome in which starting from the beginning and until the end, it is akin to zero-sum game. In other words, the businessman nurtures high-intensity desires that aim quicker realization of ends, either through minimization of necessary steps or through increase in the effectiveness of the means that could be deployed. Let us use the term $\bar{D}$ for intensified desire fulfillment, as against $\bar{d}$ for typical desire fulfillment, the term we used to betoken realization of the desired ends in usual course of everyday life. The fisherman is fishing simply for his living, and he is neither looking for alternative to his fishing activity nor any new methodology to execute his fishing routines in any different ways. In other words, he is in $\bar{d}$-fulfillment mode, seeking desire fulfillment with his mind bound-up in constancy of ethics–abundance consciousness. It is, however, true that the infusion of present-day methods could expand his horizon of possibility, but this could also change the nature of his fishing activity in a completely different way. The businessman could deploy contemporary methods and easily do many other things with the time he spends otherwise just for performing the act of fishing. But, that could also render him vulnerable to the possibility of remaining out of being in the world, unlike the fisherman, due to incessant engrossment of his mind with the idea of missing something, the idea of scarcity. In essence, the race of incessant thoughts could transfigure the businessman's mind from one smaller circle of engagement (CoE) to the yet bigger CoE, with beginning and end remaining identical like before. Movement to bigger circle is what the businessman dubs progress. The fisherman on the other hand is also active, albeit in a unique-to-himself-suited CoE, without the idea of scarcity in his mind, and this is the keynote. Fisherman's engagement in his uniquely proportioned CoE is for $\bar{d}$-fulfillment and not an absent-minded indulgence in $\bar{D}$-fulfillment. In this way, he protects himself well against the exposure to heightened entropy around him compared to his businessman counterpart.

Hence, while the businessman leisurely fishes, his mind is engaged in successively higher entropy CoE, which leaves him trapped in a hula hooping dance routine where he must shake unabated to stay therein. In other words, just to stay contemporary, he must accelerate relentlessly on the so-called slippery slope of progress. Therefore, it is not only a promise of uniqueness that drives him to increase the tempo of his activities, but the highly dynamic nature of the contingent environment around him that compels him to do what he does—keep circling—rustling and bustling!

Being in Past–Present–Future

The idea of relationship between past, present, and the future is quite different for both businessman and fisherman. For the businessman, the future CoE is radically distinct from each of the present CoEs—for him, there is no present CoE—it is either the future CoE or the ante-future CoE. The ante-future CoE is just the past for him. And, whichever CoE businessman is in, is not his present CoE, as he is never there in his mind! Therefore, in pursuit of $\bar{D}$-fulfillment, his past and future are disconnected with his present CoE by default and not by his choice. On the other hand, the fisherman coursing within the same CoE knows what to expect from the future on the basis of his past experience—all by his choice and not by default. Horizon of expectation from the future and the space of experience in past, are broadly congruent for the fisherman, but maximally distinct for the businessman. The latter, cut-off from present and past is coercively drawn into future, a yet-to-be-valid realm of time. Therefore, he constructs an entirely different concept of chronology that is unreal and constrained in scarcity.

Being in Time and Phenomenon

For Rosa's businessman, time is finite, therefore linear and scarce. He tries to maintain control over his present time, but ignores it altogether and instead plans scrupulously for a non-existent future time. Therefore, the more dynamic he becomes with his time as a whole, the more unfulfillable his desires become in the present time. The propensity of his desires to continually move to an ever larger CoE assigns him to a vectorial phenomenon and besets him to transform again and again in anticipation of his $\bar{D}$-fulfillment. Therefore, in terms of end-state measures, the businessman becomes like the fisherman again, who by his choice has declined to alter his future to any intensified desire fuelled scheme of things. For the fisherman, time is circular in the nature of repeating itself, but all in the domain of present time. In other words, (business-) man, assigned in a linear time phenomenon experiences scarcity and (fisher-) man, engaged in circular time discerns abundance, where past, present, and the future times are interlinked in the continuum of constancy and ethics–abundance principle, see Figure 3.1.

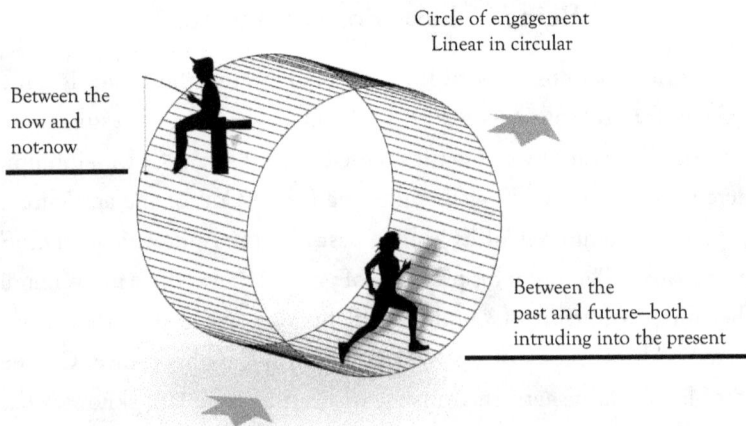

Circle of engagement
Linear in circular

Between the
now and
not-now

Between the
past and future—both
intruding into the present

Figure 3.1 Businessman and fisherman

Therefore, manner of man's being in the world depends a great deal on the temporal phenomenon he deals with—he could of course desire to live in a certain way to meet certain ends. However, the quality of his time in the measure of scarcity or abundance is overtly not at his disposal. Temporal phenomena have a common-ness character and therefore act as the given fact of time. They have a direct and deterministic influence on man's speed of being in the space–time domain. Speed of processes and events around the man is fundamental to his everyday existence. However, as we read about the fisherman–businessman story, the cause and the mode of expression of speed could be completely diverse for them from their respective standpoints.

Temper of Speed and Temperament of Man

In the act of human perspicacity, man experiences speed at all three levels of his personality, albeit in contrasting ways. At an animative—the bio-gaia body—personality level, speed is experienced in terms of change in method of action; at a cognitive—the mind—personality level, speed is experienced as fluctuations occurring in pace of everyday life, and at the normative—the intellect—personality level, speed is experienced as alterations transpiring in everyday norms of living. As a result, speed has direct and fundamental influence over the decision-making process of man in the milieu of his everyday life. In other words, man could comprehend the temper of speed at all three of his personality levels, see Figure 3.2.

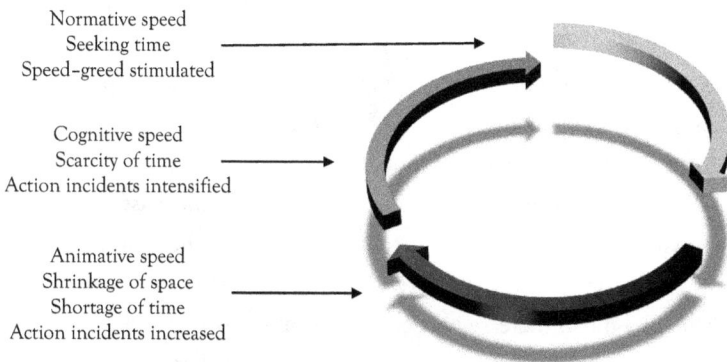

Normative speed
Seeking time
Speed-greed stimulated

Cognitive speed
Scarcity of time
Action incidents intensified

Animative speed
Shrinkage of space
Shortage of time
Action incidents increased

Figure 3.2 Temper of time and temperament of man

A. Animative (linear) speed: In order to fulfill his desires, man willfully intervenes to identify and deploy contemporary methods to accelerate his actions to attain the desired outcomes and thereby sets up a speed dynamic within his bio-gaia body. And, as the desire is intense ($\bar{D}$-fulfillment), the commensurate speed is linear and animatedly affirmative—and its effect is time-bearing with direct correlation with space within the fundamental space–time relationship. In other words, the increase in speed brings about a corresponding compression of distance or space. In this scenario, experience of space is a function of the length of time it takes to traverse it, and space, therefore, gets obliterated by time due to speed. As more free time or surplus time is released due to shrinkage of space or lesser time being required to perform activities, he tends to include more activities in his schedule of present time. Thus, every shrinkage of space due to increase in animative speed triggers a reinforced feeling of shortage of time. In other words, animative speed has an intentional overtone of chasing $\bar{D}$-fulfillment, and paradoxically, it sets up an ongoing feeling of shortage of time with an ever-increasing count of action incidents in his everyday schedule of living.

B. Cognitive (oscillating) speed: Unlike animative speed, in the cognitive course of speed, there is no distance that has to be covered faster—contrastively, on the other hand, it is to be covered more frequently. The phenomenal mind is goal-directed, hence a linear processor, whereas noumenal mind is an oscillatory processor. Therefore, it is an oscillatory speed experienced in a mind vacillating between to-do and not-to-do judgment points. Cognitive speed is induced by an intensification of action incidents due to heightened animative speed and the resultant cognitive experience per unit of time. Impact of such intensified action incidents to be manifested in a future time as $\bar{D}$-fulfillment is compared with relevant memories of similar action incidents that took place in past time. And, because the mind oscillates between future and the past, its temper is oscillatory and assimilatory. Cognitive speed is stimulated either due to a direct increase in speed of action or corresponding decrease in blank times between activities. The overall impact is seen in terms of heightened pace of action incidents, either due to an increase in supplementary action incidents to catch up with the time or to lever-age time rendered free as a result of increase in the animative speed of action incidents. Since *thought,* being non-material, is out of bounds of physical laws, every measure of increase in animative speed dis-proportionately enhances and skews the experience of cognitive speed. Cognitive speed simulates a feeling of scarcity of time, i.e., time moving faster and, therefore hastens another spell of increased animative speed expressed via an increased effort to introduce new methods to execute subsequent action incidents.

C. Normative (circular) speed: Normative speed relates to the rate of change in norms of living—both quantitatively and qualitatively—to invigorate an evolving relationship between man and the phenom-ena around him. In the relatively stable and finite element of present time, there is congruence between space of experience and horizon of expectation for the (fisher-) man. Therefore, in this timeframe, the two ends are palpable in the sphericity or the whole-ness of circular time, whereby the (fisher-) man could refer to his past to evaluate the quasi-stable present and passably hypothesize his future by itself. In the present time, therefore, the experiences and learning processes of man do have an action orienting power, and his desires do find a certain measure of proxy fulfillment. However, as sequencing of the past, present, and future is unlikely to be alike for disparate individ-uals, the individualist past could be contrasting for men in terms of value, function, and action. Hence, what remains valid for an indi-vidual within a space–time realm could be otherwise for someone else and what has already been realized here could still lie in the horizon of future somewhere else. In this way, the combined experience of present time by different men overruns the individualist experience of man and in which an extruding future of unrealized expectations at large and intruding past by way of frequent referrals to norms and standards, swamp the shrinking present of the characteristic man. In other words, the characteristic man experiences an ongoing contrac-tion of present in which temporal norms and practices are obsolet-ing faster, while at the same time, the expectations from the future are growing bigger. This also means that past and future are to be rewritten at an ever-shorter interval of time. The ongoing revision of expectation as a moving target and reconstructed experiences of the memory base are distinctive characteristics of normative speed and the cause to be for the greed–speed impulse in man who seeks and forages for time all the while.

Complex interaction of these three forms of speed constructs an intensifying scarcity of time in the present. As a consequence, humans instead of riding over the aboriginal abundance of time experience the scarcity over it. Man, as a result, begins questioning the very same ethics–abundance principle that could forge his individuality in a past-present-future continuum. Deep-seated ethical inertia that endures as the constancy of abundance consciousness behind the rapid alterations eventuating at the surface of the phenomenal world, is thus obliterated. Yet, another pattern of human identity, in terms of newer rituals, practices, and norms, precipitated by the cause of normative speed keep magnifying the already sizable void between man's scarcity and the abundance self.

Constancy: The Abundance of Timeless Time

An undifferentiated mind tends to experience time in circularity with close ends between the *now* and *not now* and in which past and future are fused together as the *other* of the present. A functionally differentiated mind, however, subsists only in a linear time conscious-ness with an open future. Human experience of time—circular or linear—could therefore be captured in a continuum out-setting with everyday time and culminating into the timeless expanse of time—the infinity—in four broad segments, see Figure 3.3.

- Everyday time (ETM): In this frame, man deals with his everyday life, for instance—recurring routines, rituals, rhythm of work time and leisure time, waking up, going to sleep, everyday schedule, and also the connected problems of synchronization, speed, duration, and sequencing of related actions. The critical issue here is the degree of routinization and habitualization with action incidents the man develops and influence they induce on his experience of living in everyday time.

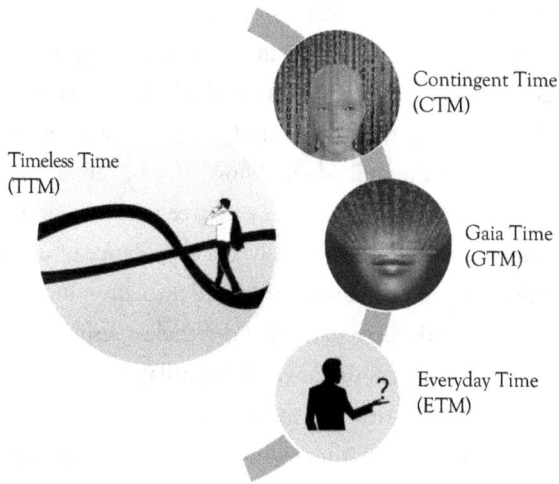

Figure 3.3 Constancy of timeless time

- Gaia time (GTM): In this frame, however, man develops a temporal perspective of life as a whole in which he reflects upon his lifetime in the context of his total bio-gaia existence. He posits his personal time in the background of sustainability of gaia time during the course of his lifetime. For example, what degrees he must earn, when and where he should buy a house and the likes, and how such decisions and actions could be sanctioned in the context of overall relationship between him as man, the animalia, and gaia, in his lifetime.
- Contingent time (CTM): In this frame, man experiences his everyday time and his lifetime, embedded in contingent time comprising fellow men of his generation and systems and cultures of his era. It is a comprehensive experience of man as a living being in which his lifetime is placed in the continuum of epoch. In this time, man evaluates his time in the context of relevant past and future as delineated by the collective man of his time. For example, beliefs, outlook, and notions, as well as temperament and moods of men of his time.
- Timeless time (TTM): Everyday time, gaia time, and contingent time are related to each other. The meaning of past, present, and future is determined simultaneously as being in

time for man, in which every present appears drowned in the
memory of past and drenched in the idea of a future. Linkage
of past, present, and future in individual life history is always
established against the background of collective life history of
men. However, the individual's knowledge of the finitude of
existence concedes to discrepancy between scarcity of limited
individual time and prospectively the abundance of unlimited
collective time to ultimately culminate into an indubitable
life problem. This discrepancy is nevertheless resolved by
the notion of timeless time, which assimilates individual
and collective life history in the expanse of collective time.
In contrast to everyday time, which is linear, quantitative,
and qualitative, timeless time is circular and attribute-less in
character. It is, thus, enduringly referenced to the constancy
of abundance.

Man allocates temporal resources at his disposal in ETM, GTM and
CTM in consideration of time required for his daily routines, his life
perspective, and his estimation of demands of time in future. All three
frames have their respective perspectives of past, present, and future and
relevance for the given action incidents. In the same way, rhythm, speed,
duration, and sequence of activities and practices are prescribed by the
collective temporal patterns and synchronization requirements of the collective man. Within the constancy of timeless time, therefore, everyday
time, lifetime, and time of the world are bound together in a meaningful whole that orients man's ethical character and conduct to make his
actions and perspectives congruent with the ethics–abundance principle.

Speed: The Scarcity of Ethical Essentia

The total human, as we contend, is one-half transient, fugitive, contingent, and the other half, enduring and unchangeable. Time manifests
through and in fragmentation of space. Contemporary time as a whole
can only be cognized as a reaction to the experience of space–time compression poked as a consequence of racing of the pace of lifetime and
extermination of space through time. A sense of impatience is formed as a

result of separation of the temporal space of experience from the horizon of expectation. Restlessness and agitation, systemic elimination of pause and absence, and categorical economization of time in the conduct of everyday time of lifetime—is attributed essentially to the scarcity mindset.

Rationalization of scarcity processes is linked to man's corroding ethical base as a consequence of overly fast changes overlapping his norms of living. As a result of the high normative speed, ethical rules of interdependence erode before new modes of integration have enough time to form and establish in everyday time of the man. Therefore, change and increasing differentiation *per se* are not the problem for man, but their too fast tempo is a drag in which nothing could retain its preceding meaning.

Scarcity triggers high-intensity desires ($\bar{D}$-fulfillment) that aims quicker realization of ends through either minimization of necessary steps or an increase in effectiveness of the means employed by man. These means invariably tend to ignore ethical norms and therefore subjected to low ethics inertia. Life's tempo changes the accessible ideational content of consciousness per unit of time. The essence of scarcity is experiencing and interpreting the world in accordance with fixed contents of the individual self, one in which the fluid element of the collective self gets completely dissolved in gradual degrees. It is a shift in balance between speed of movement and inertia of ethics in favor of the former and thus also the dissolution of natural rhythms of life in favor of portending change.

Speed and Quantitative–Qualitative Individuality

There is an increase of quantitative individuality and, simultaneously disappearance of original qualitative individuality as a result of subordination of subjective human before the objective man. On the one hand, processes of ever-finer differentiation are accompanied by parallel growth of global chains of interdependence and, on the other, unity and coherence of the whole society seem to disappear in the wake of ever-increasing differentiation. Antecedent of speed is no doubt the dynamic of desire ($\bar{D}$-fulfillment), as we contend. The unfulfilled agenda of the human strikes dynamism in desires and all human actions are accordingly initiated. The gaia nature of man, however, constantly attempts to resettle the entropy thus created through his mis-actions. Just as the process of individualization propagates in waves and does not transpire evenly or continuously, so too the dynamic movement of gaia nature is in the form of waves. Speed cannot be apprehended until there is an unmoving of dynamic stability. Only when speed and ethics-inertia coalesce at a balancing point, does time abandon its chronical characteristic and submits itself to an abiding constancy of abundance.

Exterior–Interior Inertia

There is a natural limit to speed of an animated body and stimulus-processing speed of the mind. There is also a limit to the tempo of reproduction of natural raw materials—capacity of earth's ecosystems to process toxic substances and waste materials. One can also sense slowdown as a dysfunctional side-effect of differential system speed—a traffic jam or unemployment due to employees unable to keep pace with the production tempo etc. Furthermore, there is inertia of ideology in terms of longing for a lost world of calm, stability, and leisure. Therefore, at whatever cognitive speed that man is, over time, he gathers supplemental speed and eventually starts accelerating to which ethics could be the only psychological brake. Ethics-inertia, thus, decelerates the objective movements—animative as well as cognitive—while maintaining dynamism of the mind in the constancy of abundance.

A highly developed mind pre-supposes a high constancy in the validity of collective consciousness. Dynamic humans put themselves at risk from rapid obsolescence of their tradition base that complements their dynamism. In order to cope with this, sustenance of declining traditional resources, whose validity demonstrates constancy, become all the more important. In other words, there seem to be limits to the capacity of man to process change, and the element of ethics-inertia is necessary for coexistence of man with the accompanying gaia system in the phenomenal world. This apparent slowdown is not opposed to the speed dynamic as such—on the contrary, it represents an internal element and the inherent complementary principle of the phenomenon of speed itself. This is not the speed-breaker, but a balancing-inward speed dynamic so as to qualitatively enhance the speed dynamic in terms of its stability and sustainability.

Contingency and Constancy: The Slippery Slopes

Unrest or transformative entropy within is a unique characteristic of the bio-gaia system. There is no stable or long-term aggregate state or any fixed connection of man with anything or anyone in the phenomenal world—no link with any principle is conspicuously detectable. When the normative speed reaches a higher tempo than the basic sequence of contingent time, one may conjecture serious consequences for intergenerational relations. Change is no longer perceived as transformation of a fixed mindset, but as fundamental and potentially chaotic indeterminacy. With a shrinking present, man tends to be in *period relationships* rather than *lifelong relationships*—*period identities* rather than *lifelong associations*. It could pertain to personal relationships or even group identities—the consciousness of contingency in man's ties in the world is being heightened. The awareness that things could be otherwise, not only through someone else's choices but also through one's own pick, and the resulting uncertainties and compulsions to justify inertia therefore increase.

From a phenomeno-logical perspective, speed or the ensnared greed to fulfill intensified desire ($\bar{D}$-fulfillment) alters the relationship of man with space, time, things, and even other beings in a way that his being in the world is characterized by the perception of standing—in all areas of life—on slippery slopes. The scarcity mind compels man to relentlessly shift to ever bigger CoE of intensified activities, shrinking his present even further. With every shift to a bigger CoE, focus of scarcity mind advances further into future time, and the reference point for validation intrudes yet deeper into the past time. If man does not continually re-adapt to steadily shifting conditions of action, he eventually loses connections that could enable all his future options. Result is indubitably a permanent reformation of the decision landscape that not only devalues his principle base and temporal experiences, but also makes it almost impossible to predict which connections and opportunities for action will be relevant and important for him in the future time. Wherever it becomes difficult to foresee relevancies of action incidents in relation to $\bar{D}$-fulfillment, a natural reaction is to attempt to keep open as many options as possible—or even all of them—for later realization. This is temporalization of complexity, which in turn, induces further accelerating both

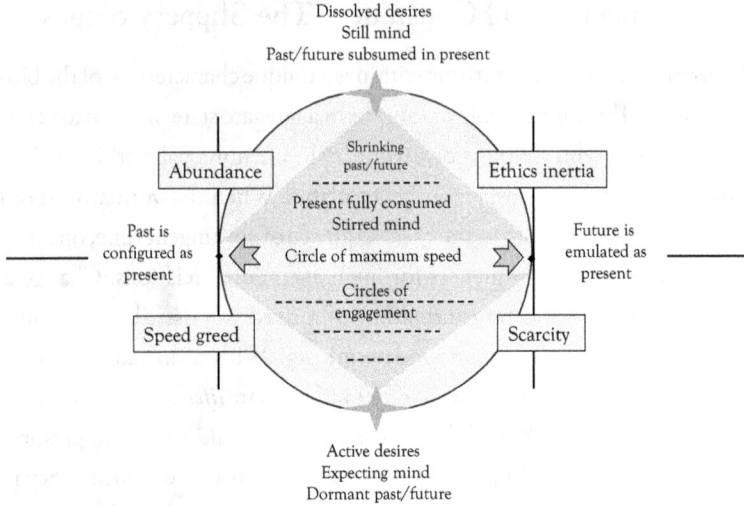

Figure 3.4 The slippery slopes

physically and psychologically and further shrinking present time, see Figure 3.4.

Only recourse to halt the greed–speed phenomenon of scarcity is to tame desires through *stilling of mind* and focus on need optimization, instead of greed maximization with the help of a perfectly aligned mind–intellect instrument connected with the abundance of collective consciousness. Man must cull his need for time in the context of collective time of his era. It is only when desires are plugged into bio-gaia needs of man that mind could recapture its natural rhythm of abundance consciousness. Overly propped up desires dissolve in the now—the moments of truth—a phrase used by Jan Carlzon, then CEO of Scandinavian Airlines System (SAS) as the title of his book, *Moments of Truth (1985)*, where he has presented the profile of abundance leadership that helped SAS to emerge from deficit to profitability, improved services, and enhanced market position—and normalize to more inclusive coexistence of man with the gaia dynamic of his times. Mind is then absorbed back into the abundance of present time, as future and past times begin to merge into it, maintaining a perfect balance by virtue of ethics inertia, see Figure 3.5.

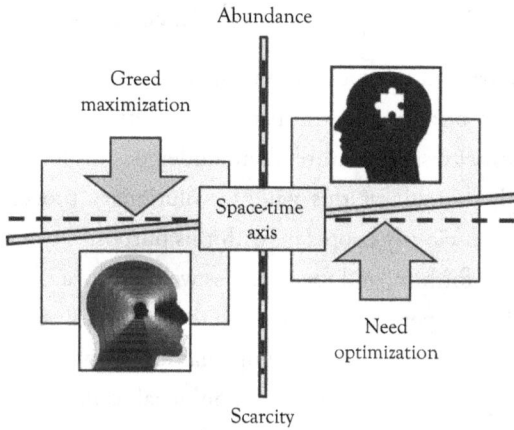

Figure 3.5 Need–greed co-action

The Corona Effect: Freed-Up Time Stress

Pace of life postulates an intensification of action incidents and the resultant experience thereof per unit of time, and it could manifest in four different ways—action becomes faster—idle time between action incidents is reduced—several actions are performed simultaneously as in multitasking—slow activities could be replaced by faster ones. The decision-making process, therefore, becomes even more complex in view of the various options that arise ever more frequently within the course of everyday life and therefore consume more time because the consequence of decisions and their interdependencies become unforeseeable and force one to expend more and more on greed-impaired acquisition.

Intensification of life's pace, thus, represents a reaction to scarcity of time resource, in the sense that for a particular action or experience, there is less time available than before. Men do not have a clue to what to rationally do with the immense reserve of freed-up time—the Corona effect! Man has time only to the extent of a finite lifetime in which he has to experience the change in him and to acknowledge the worth of time he deploys in action incidents toward $\bar{D}$-fulfillment. Others evaluate him on the basis of time they have spent with him, which is quite different than his experience with himself in the same period and its linkage with his total lifespan.

Evolution Through Involution

Evolution is truly a progressive manifestation of perfection already involved in the creation. In the backdrop of uncaused and collective abundance consciousness, nature alone undergoes evolutionary change. Man is simply a result of this willful evolutionary process of nature. If man could consciously cooperate with this purposive will of nature, so much the better for him, and for nature as well. Ethics and morals operationalize willing cooperation of man with this superordinate intent or the will of nature. In other words, phenomenal reality, which is always in a state of flux, is just a surface play upon noumenal reality, perfectly aligned to the ethics–abundance principle, which is consistent and constant. True knowledge is one by which man can realize the one constant projecting itself through inexhaustible variations. Circularity is whole—linearity is not. Faster you run, greater is the demand for solidity and stability of your feet on the plane you run. Abundance, thus, argues that change cannot be managed well in terms of change alone—constancy of the polestar in the sky is imperative for safe navigation on the sea. Abundance could only be experienced in the infinite within the subjective self of the man. For this, the mind must *still* and turn inwards to be aware of its subjective self and realize its collective self in the abundance of infinite dimension. The pursuit of self-actualization through greed maximization must yield to self-realization through need optimization. That is what call, the evolution through involution, see Figure 3.6.

Value Foundations of Constancy

Throughout life, man remains engrossed in dazzling display of magical feats, never for a moment perusing to understand the magician incognito. On the contrary, he attempts to unravel tricks of the magician on his own—and in that, he errs and falters. Instead, if he had sought to understand the magician, first, he could have received the right insights about that magic without wasting unnecessary time or energy. Opting to focus on the magic rather than the magician is the underlying cause of man's ethical dilemma relating to probing the bio-gaia system and his existence within through sundry man-made instruments and structures. Behind

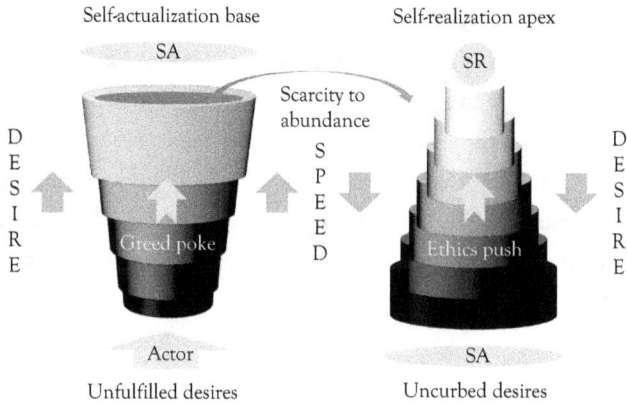

Figure 3.6 Involution to evolution

the assortment and change of acts, a magic show persists the unity and constancy of the magician. To realize this truth beyond the realm of reason—or the domain of intellect—as the intrinsic core of being, our ethical conduct is an imperative. The unchangeable, the whole, the permanent is at the base and at the core of all changes, all parts, and all transients—not just in terms of theoretical speculation at the level of reason, but also as a realized fact at the level of feeling. Commitment of man to this choice is of futuristic significance to both values and ethics.

It is important to recognize that to design and create a complete, stable, and lasting business of collective and individual existence in society—based on constancy underlying the change, requires incalculable creative labors of the selfless selves. If change does not always remind men and take them back forever to the anchor of intrinsic freedom and constancy, then it is both individualistically and collectively harmful. Pursuits of this process by man holds the key to integral ethical-ity of men and sustainability of the bio-gaia system as a whole. This is, of course, a subjective challenge to handle objective existence of man.

As we argued, comprehending and assimilating the feel of abundance within involves *stilling* the mind by way of a dedicated discipline. In an era of brainstorming, however, the process of *mind stilling* may not be readily acceptable—change and strides toward it, however, needs to be tracked constantly. An ever-changing mind cannot be examined unless by an immutable still mind. It must, therefore, be actively recognized that the primary task of human development is to hasten and perfect this evolution in order to manifest such involved complete-ness. It is the linearity assumption of the economistic–scarcity mind, which is short term, and not the circularity assumption of the humanistic–abundance mind. It is the circular view that has the capacity to sober down our chutzpah of phenomenal linearity. Besides, the entire cosmic design is circular—earth, planets, their orbits, and so on—the concept of around-the-clock perpetuality is better captured by circularity rather than linearity.

The Key Takeaway

If we consider the essential-ity of the bio-gaia universe, then we easily end up with the idea of an unchangeable being, which suggests, through the exclusion of any increase or decrease in things, the character of its absolute constancy. If, on the other hand, we concentrate upon the formation of this essentia, then constancy is completely transcended—one form is incessantly transformed into another and the universe appends the aspect of a perpetuum mobile. This is cosmologically—and often metaphysically—interpreted as the dual aspect of being. Frenetic standstill, therefore, means that nothing remains the way it is, while at the same time, nothing essentially changes. A principle of constant surmises thus: more options that man makes available to him, less optional is the systemic framework with whose help he avails them in the first place.

CHAPTER 4

Competition Versus Collaboration

Ailment and the Aliment

As the wise saying goes, "I am also a resource to the world as everything else. Let the best from me come forth to the benefit of others as it is coming from others to me…," and, simply put, this is collective consciousness—the collaborative coexistence. Competition and collaboration both mark the value setting in our mind that drives our everyday actions. While competition is a scarcity frame that looks at world events in the bounds of finitude, collaboration is the abundance bearing of mind, which is focused inward to see the same world events in the authenticity of their primal infinite dimension. Therefore, if collaboration is a value-primed aliment to man's holistic existence, competition is a dis-value-driven ailment of his insalubrious strife.

Competitive Dis-Values and Collaborative Values

The event-focused reverse values—or rather dis-values—such as aggression, more and more, individualism, and competitive supremacy are frequent in businesses all around, as seen today. However, despite the upfront efforts toward shaping and reshaping behavior of business actors, they experience severe energy depletion at all levels in the business pecking order. Fact remains that while man is *matter and finite* on the objective plane, he is *abundant energy and infinite* on the subjective plane. The external—business or home—must be managed through internal, and not the other way round for enduring effectiveness. It is fairly incontrovertible that to mandate a good return, adequate and appropriate investment in the first place is obligatory.

As we see, it is the quality of values and the dominant and enduring tendencies of the mind that ultimately translate into man's ethical behavior. If the driving dis-values are vanity or envy, the consequential outcome must indubitably be unethical. Mind and intellect are simply instruments for triggering an action. If the direction to man comes more and more from values, the quality of his action in all likelihood is tuned ethically. This is the universal subjective dynamic, which is often ignored. No effective growth is, therefore, possible without adequate purification at the level of values and ethics, which in turn, are the emotional variables to self-sustained and inclusive growth of not only the human, but humanity as a whole. An action is not the measure of ethical values—conversely, ethical values are the measure of action. The temporal dominion must yield a big portion of its largely punitive nature to a strong and explicit ethics agenda. To do right things in the right way, man must be in connect with right consciousness—the abundance consciousness beyond the domain of mind–intellect substructure. Values and ethics coexist in a mutually reinforcing and the perennial ends-means cycle. Rules and standing orders can correct man's mistakes, but not his mis-intentions—goal of human life must be reset to ethics-centered transcendence replacing the skill-centered accomplishments.

Collaboration: The Ascent to Human Dignity

Ipso facto, it is the quality of emotions and feelings—imprudent to the intellect—that determine the legitimacy of man's mind. In the realm of decision making, therefore, it is the subjective quality of the choices made or decision undertaken, which ultimately determine the degree of objectivity, exactitude, or the equity embedded in them. In other words, subjective is the cause, objective is the effect. It is in this frequent pettiness—as opposed to dignity—that behavioral dilutions take place, and it is in the event of a dignified response that ethics-centering supervenes. Human personality is a two-layer architecture—the utilitarian, the lower individual self, and the trans-utilitarian, the higher collective self. The former is constitutionally scarcity-driven competitive self, which is conditioned, dependent, apprehensive, insecure, and hence prone to pettiness, and the latter, the abundance-soaked collaborative self, which is constitutionally ethics–abundance inspired, complete, unconditional, fearless, ever-secure, and hence, recumbent to dignity. Man's primal alienation lies in the severance within his being from the higher abundance self—every other alienation is an offshoot from here. Thus, mind, caught in the matrix of the competitive self, continues to suffer from a feeling of deficit, and most of it springs forth from comparative deprivation rather than any real deficiency per se. And, each time such feelings occur, the level of consciousness plummets further, no matter how intellectually sound the individual could be. Mischief of the downward spiral in thoughts, words, or deeds is thus set in motion.

Collaborative self is the subjective reality felt deep within the being. The now-or-never stance of man with the scarcity-driven competitive self makes him a slave to his blind impulses and he mistakes his urges, to gratify them at any cost, as the manifestation of his freedom. However, real freedom is the freedom from peonage of pettiness stemming from the mind. In collaborative self, man is the owner of his mind and not subservient to it. It is in collaborative self alone that the man could hold himself in dignity by gradually abnegating the competitive self and seeking sovereignty from it. The bearing of teamwork, dignity, sharing, cooperation, harmony, trust and the likes are all grounded in abundance and not in scarcity. In fact, the competitive self is a lone entity—just the animative self with a constrained mind. While even the most sensitive sense organs are incapable of sensing the world in entirety, completeness of the entire universe could easily be comprehended by the collaborative self. It is only in abundance that man could find every being and thing in a collaborative interrelation. The ethical self, which is deep dyed in universal collective consciousness, is antecedent to compassion and collaboration. The human flourish, which is essentially an absence of scarcity self, has a bias against the competitive self. Therefore, only when self-actualization—the objective excellence—is replaced with self-realization, the subjective perfection, do we have a universally valid principle to sustain ethical behavior. For this, a sense of guilt is eminently necessary more than pride. Completeness of the collaborative self is the antidote to scarcity-driven competitive promptings in man's behavior. The feeling-level conviction about the completeness in collaborative self enables man to take a stand, announce a decision, and execute it without the kinds of

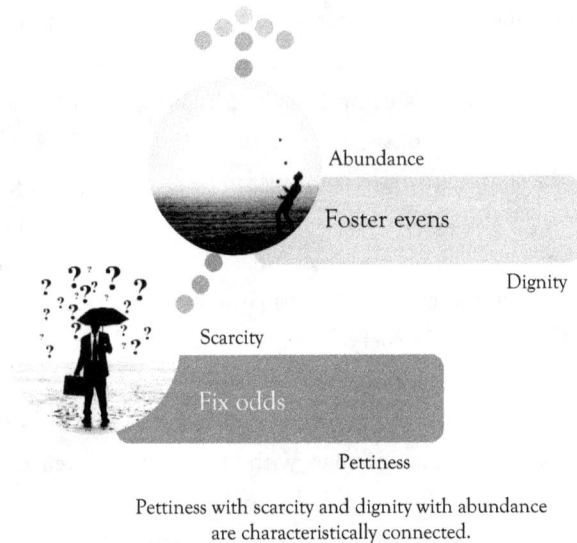

Pettiness with scarcity and dignity with abundance
are characteristically connected.

Figure 4.1 *Elements of competition and collaboration*

fear or favor to which the externally dependent competitive self is always prone. The process of living in the ethics–abundance principle is joy in itself, although external sacrifices and deprivation may invariably follow compliance of this principle.

Therefore, vital clues to the task of transformation in the context of human engagements are actually in the concept of collaborative self, when man could burst open the shell of insecure, scarcity-driven individuality and capitulate into abundance-inspired collectivity. Mind could then see a coherent construct of subjective reality, as against the disjointed assembly of objective phantasmal. The business actor could then be free from her hang-ups and conditioning and be sure of a consistent collaborative identity, which refuses to be at the mercy of the see-saw of competitive squeezing, see Figure 4.1.

Self-appraising introspection and self-examination, therefore, lay the groundwork for collaborative vision in order to handle the competitive guile of the mind. To gain this vision, man must return back to his abundance self—without detachment from scarcity self, there can be no collaborative vision or integrative intelligence. The methodical psychological process of deep rhythmic breathing, emptying, and *stilling the mind* in slow degrees and such other steps are, therefore, indispensable and essential to see the totality of abundance. Man is not because he thinks—on the contrary—he thinks because he is. In other words, thinking is an effect, and not the cause. The journey of competitive self to collaborative self is a realization of the vital distinction between the owner and the owned within a more comprehensive concept of abundance self. We need to dictate the mind and not be dictated by it and dictate it through the autonomous anchor that is abundance self—thus alone could man neutralize the decline of abundance-oriented ethical behavior. The only non-competitive route to success, ambition, and desire fulfillment ($\bar{d}$ or $\bar{D}$) is the search for completeness in abundance. As the search progresses, his competitive self begins to function in ways which he generally wishes to see in behavior of others toward him. In the beginning, the idea of completeness could appear abstract and unseen, much like the mathematics or physics. However, working from the plane of collaborative self, man could assuredly see the unity in diversity. A better man must first realize the best human within him. Finite individualization must be seen in the context of infinite collectivization for the sustainability of all things and beings in a collaborative framework. The idea of individualization and differentiation must be understood in the light of the truth that the competitive man is an entity in temporary disengagement from collaborative unity, by way of differentiation and to be back to the same unity by way of association with collective consciousness at some point or other.

Sustainability and Competition

As the moral moorings of man-the-actor construct his composite fortitude, the transformation of this actor alone could prompt collective transformation, and nothing could be more central to transformation of man-the-actor than his own actions themselves. This transformation, however, must crystallize in the crucible of his everyday deeds—his everyday work. In the frantic race for material competition, however, there is the danger of adopting an algorithmic view of transformation of the business actor. Hope seems to be that a transformed actor will be more productive, create more profits, and thus lift the business back to the peak once again. However, economistic or pecuniary or objective development is not enough and not even sustainable. The real transformation mantra must be the subjective development of the actor—the development of man's bio-gaia maintainability in the infinite of self-sustained abundance. Objective growth has a foreordained glass ceiling—the highly unstable plane of self-actualization as the best possible upshot. Those really concerned with the future of not only the man and material systems but also humans and the indispensable gaia system, need to muster enough courage to grasp the nettle of need-based simple living and support-n-sustain based high thinking. The struggle, therefore, is to be between how much the man could possess versus how little he could live on. Replenishment and rejuvenation of the gaia system is the fundamental substratum over which man's growth story could be developed, matured, maintained and sustained. Those who could train themselves to live on less and control themselves well with the overall sustainability of bio-gaia ordering would eventually win the battle of scarcity.

Collaborative consciousness is the one inexhaustible source for all resources. When humans progress toward experiencing the collaborative consciousness within, their external needs and yearnings begin to diminish. Greed fueled, externalized, competitive, and economistic battle starts losing its pretentious relevance—sanity begins to return, and assaults on the bio-gaia system are eased. This perspective of coexistence and sustenance of bio-gaia itself is a transformation worth keeping in focus. Pursuit of abundance—the collaborative consciousness—is the intended end, not the means-to-end. And, the values, vision, stability, and so on to stay ahead of competition are just the underwriting of greed fulfillment $(\bar{D})$—nothing more. Strength, freedom, and peace at work cannot come to anxious, calculating, comparing, and scarcity-driven mind—structures and systems have no fundamental answers to offer here. Erudition deals with rational self in the head—collaborative self alone can work upon both, the mind and the consciousness. The ethics at work is the one distinctive freedom-yielding route that works, inside out. Empowerment and attunement flowing from abundance is, thus, the original, the holistic, and the effective.

Creativity, Sustainability, and Collaborative Consciousness

If creativity at work does not conform to collaboration and the ethics–abundance principle, then it could hardly be transformational in nature. Free will, source of any creative impulse, could be variegated uttermost to the stretch of ROYGBIV if man's focus is slanted to the narrow color range within the sweep of this variegation. However, when ocular diversification in the band of colors gets dissolved, a scrupulous and colorless light emerges with all possibilities and fullest creativity subsumed within it. Therefore, it is only when the competitive self is submerged into the abundance of collaborative consciousness and assumes the collective dimension of existence, creativity could become real, alive, and continual. And, as against the scampering in finite world with a greed and speed disposition, man could grow with a sense of unity in the region of self-sustained collaborative consciousness. Therefore, unless creativity on the phenomenal plane can proceed from the primal and abundant source of creativity on the noumenal plane, it is bound to remain fretful, error-prone, and a temporary dazzle. The inevitable creative tendency, in absence of such anchoring, would only be to idealize the objective-real instead of realizing the subjective-ideal. This could be the real challenge of collectivism and the very idea of abundance. A sustainable future of the bio-gaia planet and humanity necessarily calls for unity with collaborative consciousness and collectivity in all humans. It must be keenly examined if man's proliferation is reinforcing centralization, complexity, and magnitude, or it is edifying simplicity, inclusivity, and contentment—simply because harmony, balance, and inner self-fulfillment in a human relationship peg on the latter and the thrust of human creativity must be directed to that. Man must, therefore, shift his domain from simply doing the creative work to thoroughly perfecting in ethical work and from simply being engaged in calculable routine to being immersed in lustrating work.

Human maturation must place the man in an abundance setting and guide, from that ascendancy, his concerns and tasks. If vocation is going to be the dominant form of avocation as well, it must get involved in renewing an authentic outlook toward collectivization and not just individualization. Goals cannot be just material or economic.

Economics must gear up to serve the collective human end. The subjective art of human work, therefore, lies in aligning itself with the ethics–abundance principle, the collaborative consciousness, the oneness of humans, and singularity of life as such. Passage from the realm of necessity to the realm of freedom from necessity, lies in man's efforts toward individual selfless work. Along with experimentations, therefore, the business actor must get down to introspection, reflection, and unadulterated observation as well.

For long, scarcity maxim has been proclaiming that competitive spirit is the key to success or excellence—where and how to attack a *competitor* is the prominent highlight of such a strategy discourse in economics and commerce in modern times. And, yet, the well instructed in management talk of cooperation, systemic interdependence, and even business ethics! The contradictions between *attacking* competition and *ethical* business cannot stay unrecognized for long within the overall strategy framework. The scarcity maxim erroneously terms *higher standards of consumption* as *higher standard of living*. The former is objective and can be measured, the latter is subjective and can only be felt—between the two, there is hardly any positive correlation. The scarcity maxim tends to interpret progress only in terms of a perpetual change. The notion of destination and stability is alien to it. The operational approach tends to become an endless series of old fallacies replaced with new fallacies. And, it is this game of fallacies in succession that is deemed progress. Thus, the scarcity maxim just breeds an exponential series of change adding up to harum-scarum of confusion and abetting just bewilderment.

The ethics–abundance principle, on the other hand, insists on a self-existent core of collaborative human flourish in measureless and collective coexistence. That which is permanent cannot undergo mutation. Also, there cannot, in principle, be mutable phenomenon without an immutable noumenon. Progress, therefore, lies in circumventing the changing phenomenal exposition and experiencing the unchanging noumenal reality—this is the destination. Streams of water, after merging and settling into the river, are not exterminated. Brilliant tricks of a magician are so enthralling that none in the audience feel the urge to know the magician himself. The show is over, they leave the theater with light-hearted fulfillment. The bio-gaia system, at the universal level, also suffers similar treatment at the hand of the scarcity maxim, which gets lost in unraveling the mysteries and the magic of creation. Since creation is endless, this knowledge is also endless. The ethics–abundance principle dares to go backstage to know the creator, the magician—the abundance of uncaused cosmic energy.

The scarcity maxim prods the mind to commit a basic theoretical error in trying to prepare the man for managing his affairs exclusively in terms of finites and parts—a circumscribed, rigid, objectivized framework that excludes the whole, the infinite. The ethics–abundance principle, on the other hand, enjoins management of finites without an awareness and a feel for the infinite is bound to create a chaotic situation in rather unexpected ways. Taming impure emotions like, jealousy, pride, anger, arrogance, and greed, though natural, must therefore, be attempted in as much earnest as we attempt to break away from autogenetic gravity in order to land on mars in a claim to human progress. When a righteous battle for universal flourish is waged as a last preferred choice without petty personal venom or self-enoblement as the driving impulse, it is worth fighting. This is simply because, in collective flourish alone, is individual happiness guaranteed—this is the collaborative mindset. Therefore, it is with reason that man must understand that collaborative consciousness along the ethics–abundance principle has its ground in something beyond reason. It is rather outlandish that while man has no difficulty in understanding the concept of pure food, pure water, and pure everything material around him, yet that the idea of a pure mind confounds him assiduously!

To Change! or to Transform!

Change must be addressed in a rather matter-of-fact way and laid bare to see if it is transformational or it is just transmutation. Therefore, the three indispensable questions pertaining to the energy–matter–time balance of the bio-gaia system must be asked:

1. As a result of the no holds barred ambition, is he, the man, tenanting precariously close to the nadir of inadequacy and scarcity of primal

gaia matter itself—and has not disrupted the balance of matter in the bio-gaia system as a result of his flimsy commitments, shifting preferences, and onslaught of fragmenting changes eventuating all around him?

2. What hope could he cohere from ongoing and high-speed changes—as a result of time imbalance—dissembling around him purportedly to lift him out of the mess that he is manufacturing around him?

3. What does he secure from these changes, goaded by a mind that is afflicted with slavery disguised as freedom, to uplift his collective spirit and restore the primordial integrative energy balance of the bio-gaia system as a whole?

So, what is the real intent behind the all-out competition and changes it triggers? What will be its consequence in relation to the sustainability of the bio-gaia system and the humanity itself? Changes, as such, cannot be opposed, and yet, before any change is attempted, a few basic and ultimate questions about the sustainability of the bio-gaia scheme and humanity must be asked—how could man gain real freedom wearing the debilitating pain of an unabated corona admonition? If fearless scrutiny of past changes, and their adverse consequences at a macro level in managing the bio-gaia system leads to nonlinear conclusions, then the strategies for future change should be completely re-examined and altered. All varieties of economic activities should gear the processes of change toward helping man to achieve his essence in completeness, by and through collaboration at work—there is just no other way he could transcend scarcity into the abundance of collective human flourish.

If concern for the ultimate meaningful-ness of life is man's truly dominant motive, then his individual goal must also be linked to the collective and superordinate human goal. This alone can help man survive with dignity and strength, despite the inevitable vagaries in the throes of change. Change must be yoked, in principle, to the unchanging universal abundance consciousness. Boundaries that must really become fluid are those between individual quest and collective conquest. It is by the pursuit of only such long-term agenda that man could self-realize his multidimensional abundance self beyond the unidimensional scarcity self.

Competition, Excellence, and Ethics

It is supremely essential that man's mind must strive to regain contact with its ground state of collaborative consciousness—from ceaseless exteriorization to circadian interiorization—from complex living to simple living—from outer-objective innovation to inner-subjective discovery—from competitive survival of the fittest to cooperative sustenance of all—from greed-and-grab to need-and-cede—from mindless speed to mindful constancy—from phenomenal individual-ism to noumenal collective-ism—from arithmetical networking to spontaneous connecting—from nature as my resource to nature as my source—from seeking freedom to securing freedom—from scarcity mind to abundance consciousness. Once this essential aim becomes the first concern of human development efforts, man could be commensurately assured that his objective conditions of existence will spontaneously fall into an integrated collaborative pattern.

In the context of ethics–abundance, the basic idea behind excellence is to excel through self-competing and not competing with others—recall our discussion on the reverse polarity of ACE motor that could transmute compete-with-others leaning into compete-with-self sensibility once the focus of man is entrained inward into his own being. If this leads to excelling over another, then that is a mere by-product, a secondary phenomenon. Competition, especially interpersonal, often proves to be a precarious and psychological zero-sum game. The stressful dissipation of energy caused by the dis-values fostered by this spirit is colossal. In competitive skirmishes, excellence is invariably not the real objective. Instead while manifesting the best, often, the worst is exposed. In the truest sense, human excellence, as already embodied in man's collaborative personality, comprises five of his character elements, see Figure 4.2:

1. Collective character personated at an elevated ethics–abundance position

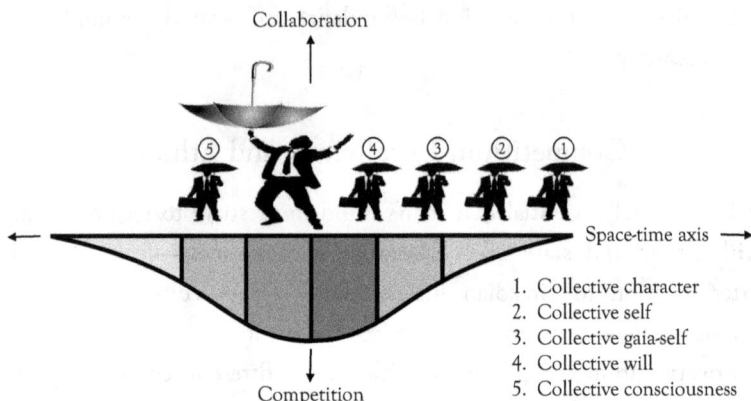

Figure 4.2 The collaborative personality

2. Collective self that serves collective endeavors and goal
3. Collective gaia self for universal sustenance of beings and things
4. Collective will to be expressed in all actions
5. Collective consciousness pursuing human flourish

Therefore, if collaborative pursuit is the ultimate foundation and highest conception of ethics–abundance, then competition is certainly not essential for excellence. In fact, competition would be a barrier against progress towards collective human flourish, and because of this barrier, infractions of ethics–abundance codes will tend to proliferate—and often enough, no real excellence could be achieved. Man to human—individual to collective—is not an effect of competition, but the after-effect of self-ascendancy! The ethical code is simply the bare commonality of collective phenomenon—tagged and cataloged in human consciousness.

Competition is, therefore, neither the cause nor the effect—it is simply waypoint—not necessary for evolution in any way. Instruments— internal mind–intellect or external tools–techniques—do not unravel the scarcity conundrum. On the contrary, the instruments simply make the man struggle even more as competition gets even keener. The containment of competition and fostering of collaborative reciprocity is the key. The thrust of the ethics–abundance postulate is meant to tone down the divisive competitive temper and drive progress upward to the integrative sense of collaboration. Real discovery is the discovery of underlined commonality of collective humanity—fragmentation is already manifested in *matter* and *time*! Anything in pursuit of collaboration is, therefore, necessarily ethical.

Recall the humanizing framework, we discussed—recovery to collective or collaborative abundance could be pursued only through a dedicated practice of done-on-purpose personal *discipline* or by way of simple *devotion* to the collective self. The path of holistic *knowledge* is the third possible track that we discussed could lead man to higher levels of understanding beyond reason. Psychological self-discipline for attainment of such understanding is, however, essential for the man in action. Collaborative existence is nothing but a subset of collective sustenance. The transcendent perspective of collaboration is the essence of ethics–abundance. As a matter of fact, man is completely immersed in competition today—it drives his plans, strategies, thoughts, and actions. From beneath the veneer, it leads to an increasing greed–speed frenzy and drives the man by fear. It is about time we realized that more the man hinges on competition-driven external standard of consumption, more mediocre will be his collaboration-secured internal standard of living. Every kind of effort on the gaia plane must, therefore, face and pass this test until it helps man to realize the immutable human flourish already present within him.

The Spirit of Collaboration

We believe that collaboration is first an ethical endeavor and, ultimately, the destination in the collective consciousness. Let us leave aside this *ultimate* plank of collaboration for the time being. Nonetheless, collaboration as an essential process of ethics–abundance framework is certainly an imperative for the man in business. Collaboration is not the in-vogue networking bug, and it is certainly not the commonplace set of behavioral manners or etiquettes. Managing self in ethics–abundance is, therefore, an education in character building and not a training to whet social politesse and civic urbanity. And, unless such education is planned earnestly and undertaken wholly right from the early years in man's life as the principal agendum for his future, the spirit of collaboration will continue to evaporate out from the midst of human life. The spirit of collaboration, therefore, stands for the collectivity and the interconnectedness of men in a universal setting. It is an assimilation and a unique demeanor that implies progressive enlargement of the subjective frame of reference for work. While dominion laws, rules, and regulations are necessary all the time, the empathic collaborative–cooperative mooring is must for man's progress to attain the collective human flourish.

Collaborative Ethics: The Future Horizon

The widespread and dominant assumption in business disposition today is that fully permissive and liberal competition will promote ethics at work. While this could be true in certain specific circumstances in unqualified times, the real long-term solution lies in moving beyond the mixed effects of competition upon work ethics, towards a more reassuring collaborative yearning. However, collaboration must rest on spirit-collaboration and not on form-collaboration. It is, therefore, important to understand the fundamental difference between spirit and form. Human being with a well-formed individual self at the heart of her scarcity personality attempts to invariably convert virtually everything to some kind of self-advantage. In the end, even collaboration tends to become an instrument for this self-gain tendency—this must, therefore, be the cautionary note.

Managing the manager—the individual self—should then be a task central to the process of cooperation. In an act of spirit collaboration, giving is natural and spontaneous—there is no take-for-give, there is no conjecture or indenture, no bargaining or negotiation whatsoever. The sheer feeling of collective human flourish impels and underlies all such spirit collaboration. All forms of human collaboration must maintain constant vigil on the management of the indispensable but overly complex individual self-ness. Collaboration is a way of life, a habit of the mind. It stimulates certain refined impulses and raises the ethical standards of man. All collaboration must reject man's scarcity-bound instincts of acquisition, rivalry, competition and replace them with harmony and collective consciousness on the basis of which a new economic order could be constituted.

The Key Takeaway

Man must collaborate with external-to-him to compete with internal-to-him and not the other way around. He needs to collaborate to overcome his external incompleteness and inadequacy. The thrust for competitive success is certainly fed by the separative self, though often couched in pretentious phrases like teamwork, networking, dynamic achievement drive, and so on. Consequently, across the whole spectrum from personal to business episodes, collaboration invariably takes the sub-ordinate position. This is a model of business management that does not uphold the more desirable and essential goal of collective human flourish and progress of all, but merely success for the fittest.

In contrast to such an outlook, collaboration necessarily implies containment of the augmenting self. A process of giving is more intrinsic to collaboration than appropriating. The business actor should localize her desires to her immediate environment but universalize her thoughts to a collective sense of human flourish in the spirit of collaborative abundance. Collaboration has to be a state of subjective feeling, not merely an objective thought or argument. Therefore, smaller, self-contained economic units are likely to be more intrinsically unitive and fraternal as a consequence of visible proximity. The impersonality of remote centralization is hostile to the collaborative spirit and homogenous conduct of businesses. While minimality and proximity are necessary conditions for this, they are not always sufficient. Hence, the cultivation of subjective togetherness and natural joy of giving for collective progress appears to be the indispensable theoretical foundation for any collaborative campaign.

CHAPTER 5

Ethics and Value Sensitization

Ethics and Values: Paranoia to Metanoia

To begin with, it must be clear in make-no-bones terms that rationality could simply be a habiliment to alluringly guise even the most fallacious intent, the most vindictive emotions, and the most mischievous sentiments of a scarcity mind. Since management pertains to the domain of profane rationality, utilitarian humanism—with scarcity underpinning the upper bound with material, means, and their limits—could go only as far as it could to engage the mind in unsettling pursuits. The scarcity mind works on a mulish premise that seeks material pleasure, and willy-nilly avoids labor. It is the essential nature of the greed-driven scarcity mind to maximize pleasure and material gains, and at the same time, avoid labor and associated pain. But, this is a gratuitous and untenable aberration fit only in respect of individualistic and scarcity-afflicted existence. However, in the domain of collective consciousness, this could be viewed as an opportunity in itself for deep personality transformation. The same labor and associated pain could turn inspirational, seeking no separate expression for the individual self as man's pleasure and happiness are subsumed in the flourish of collective man, the human. Ironically, desire, ambition, jealousy, and such value quirks are held out by profane rationality as the key to progress—no doubt, desire acts as the spur for emergence of individual consciousness from the uncaused collective conscience. This argument is disordered because, thereafter, man begins to get blindly caught in the web spun by his limitless desires, and he stays bound forever. The abundance principle, however, suggests a restraint on desires such that he is liberated into the state of collective consciousness, which, as we have argued, is autonomous, self-sufficient, and self-sustained. This is the sobering delineate of the ethics–abundance principle for true self-trans-formation. Even a modicum of progress in this direction will be worth-while both for the man and the human. Disciplined interiorization alone can help the man to objectively watch the twists and swerves within his mind and evaluate them sternly and subdue his insecurity and fragility.

In a sense, both the ethics–abundance principle and the scarcity maxim are insufficiency-driven. Yet, there is a whole world of difference between the two, in ways this insufficiency is felt by the man. The scarcity maxim amplifies and proliferates in the external world of yearnings of a man springing forth from a state of inner inadequacy. Hence, the man goes on multiplying his means of gratification from outside, assuming that sum of finites is infinite. But, this is the basic fumble. Deficit felt by the scarcity mind has utterly lost the capacity to experience the internal fullness and completeness of the collective consciousness. Thus, the ethics–abundance centered values lead to metanoia, while the scarcity-afflicted dis-values lead to paranoia.

Value Sourcing: State of Collective Consciousness

As we discussed, man's outer objective world is just the manifestation of his inner subjective world. There is nothing outside of him, which is not already inside him. There is nothing that has to be created—it is all there once the man is here! But, man's mind looks for everything outside and into the future. As soon as the frame of future shifts to the present, mind moves immediately to the next immediate frame in the future. So, the real present is invariably left in a state of mindlessness and the only access point—the mind—for the man to establish connect with abundance consciousness could never be established. This means, the man has lost not only access to the reservoir of amaranthine psycho-logical energy—the cosmic-energy, so vitally necessary to replenish his depleted stock of bio-gaia energy—but also lost his all-important connect with the ethics–abundance principle—the primary value source to steer him through the material and phenomenal world. In other words, both his subjective motors—balancing (PPF: past, present, future) and free-dom (IEE: involution, explore, evolution) motors—continue to remain dysfunctional, and he is left with just the objective motors—economic

(ACE: accumulate, compete, elate) and empathy (CRR: communicate, relate, reflate) motors—to deal with everyday life issues. In this way, both his energy- and value-sourcing channels are jeopardized. So, the first thing man must do is to engage with the present, dropping everything else, including his unfulfillable desires primarily pertaining to no-more-valid past or the not-yet-valid idea of the future. In other words, man must actively participate with present in the present—only then something consequential could really work out for him.

The Value Archetype

As we have argued, for ethics- or abundance-centric living, all four personality motors in man—subjective PPF and IEE as well as objective—ACE and CRR—must function efficiently in synchroneity with each other. It is only when the subjective motors are in sync with the ethics–abundance principle, could it draw upon the psychological cosmic energy through ethics–abundance values embedded in it and, in turn, drive the objective motors through the ethics–abundance value set. Also, there is a reciprocal relationship between the subjective and objective motors, in the sense that the objective dispensation of man also influences the function of subjective motors as the ever-new norms (recall our discussion on normative speed) are formed and re-registered in man's relative past—comprising his memories through his actions fueled by unfulfilled desires ($\bar{d}$ or $\bar{D}$). In this way, man's values influence his actions qualitatively and also get modified reciprocally through the same action. Therefore, it is important to examine the value archetype—the primary, the executor, the factotum, and the hightail—the fourfold value set for human conduct congruent with the ethics–abundance principle, see Figure 5.1.

The Primary: Humility in Self-Confidence

The basic calculus of humility is to see as it is and as complete as it could be within the infinite—plus and the minus. This requires prodigious self-confidence, which again could only be sourced from the abundance consciousness bypassing mind–intellect innards, that could otherwise thwart man's efforts to see things in a holistic perspective and color them

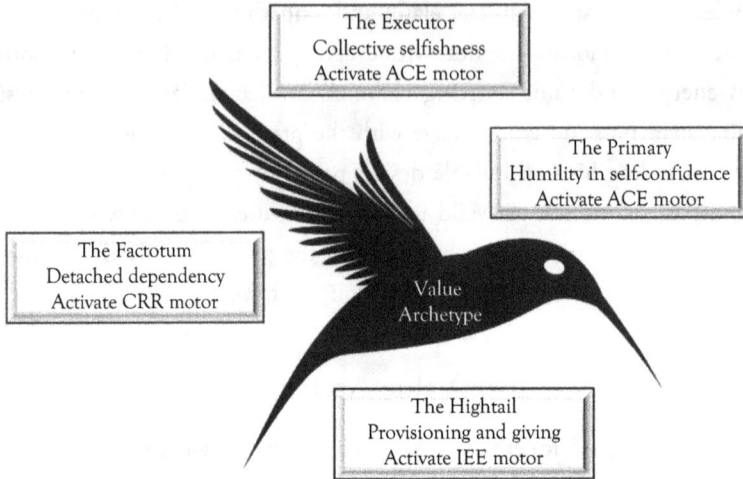

Figure 5.1 The value archetype

to their own agenda. A man with low self-confidence cannot be humble—humility is not inferiority. It is not a negative or positive self-idea—it is simply a state of *no self-idea* in which the man is fully established in the abundance of collective consciousness. A confident man could become under-confident as well, and that too very easily. If the man wants to be humble, then he must live without judging himself—without deciding what kind of personage he is. When connected with the ethics–abundance consciousness, he could perceptibly see every thought that flows within him is sourced from his self-sustained collective self. In other words, only a balanced mind with fully active PPF motor could be humble—not the one who has already arrived at a postulation.

The Executor: Collective Selfishness

The worst thing that the man could do is to try being unselfish. It is not inducible to go and work against basic human bearings—it never works out to be not natural. No doubt, unselfish-ness could be a by-product of man's dispensations, but it could never be his goal. If the man is trying to be unselfish, obviously, he believes he is not. There is a subjective human within the man, who is designed to be selfish, albeit to a collective self, and there is an objective human facing the phenomenal world, who is trying to appear unselfish through some manipulative conduct or the other all the while. It is only through this selfishness within can man truly realize that material-focused and mind-centric happiness is not the conclusive solution to his everyday challenges, and substantial effort is solicited on his part to actualize perennial happiness in his life. Real happiness could only be experienced when the mind is still and man could go beyond the mind–intellect convolution and connect with his collective consciousness, the realm of human flourish. Selfishness alone could elevate him from being an individual self to collective self. There is, however, some difference between doing what makes one happy and making demands on others to be happy—and, of course, it is not suggested here to impose any individualistic predilection on someone else. However, if man's actions do not infringe on pursuit of happiness by others, his intentions and actions to pursue happiness could be legitimate and thoroughly merited—this must, therefore, be the orientation of his ACE motor.

The Factotum: Detached Dependency

Only a strong man could be commodious for dependence on someone—the weak has no room as such for such situations. A vulnerable and fragile man would be afraid of losing control of himself in such footings. But, dependence is not the same as attachment. There is a difference between a relationship of detached dependency and an arrangement of convenience—although there is nothing wrong about latter, but there is nothing right about it either. In a downright relationship, no doubt, man could go through his jealousy, his anger, his frustration, his possessiveness, and practically, every other emotional peril and exploit. In fact, it is only because he has all these in the first place that he is separated from his primordial collective self and be an individual self. Therefore, it is naturally needed for him to go through these emotions instead of pretending that they do not exist—merely closing one's eyes cannot dispel fear as a cat would like believe! If man does not get jealous, it does not mean he is beyond jealousy—it could also mean that he has not been in a situation where he could become jealous! To experience unconditional love in any relationship, one must first love even with attachment and all possible conditions, and then earnestly try to go beyond attachment and each one of such conditions. This is how the CRR motor must be attuned, else the very same love could turn into hatred once the conditions of love are gone. While growing, life could become challenging—unsettled in some way or other. Nevertheless, wherever there is attachment, there is certainly the possibility of some sort of emotional churn taking place. While detachment sounds good, it is not palsy-walsy to make it happen. It does not feel good handling an about-face even when it finally happens!

The Hightail: Provisioning and Giving

It must be acceded unmistakably that the archetypal human being in a sustainable and living bio-gaia system must be closer to the self-restrained sort rather than the self-exorbitant assort. Man could thrive in nature, only when he is just nature like—the *giving* type—to provide for his individual self as well as the collective self. But, giving is not the simple act of physical giving of the gross objects. The key element of giving is the spirit of humility in dissolving the give-and-take material desire and hankering to fulfill any reciprocal commitment. And, for this, the IEE motor must be fully activated, and man must work hard with dedication to neutralize the rights-oriented greed–speed impulses within the desire-smacked mind.

There is no denying that an overzealous and greed–speed driven economistic streak fosters a gain-n-grab momentum across the pecking order in the system and structure. In the first place, this stance provokes man's unethical conduct even further and his relationship with nature all together—inevitably followed by a virtually uncontrollable flood of ethical disturbances in relationships with his fellow men across the system and structure. Therefore, scarcity-afflicted greed and rivalry for external objects must be gradually replaced with enduring internal fullness and completeness. The spirit of giving springs forth from abundance consciousness. It is important to absorb that giving is posterior to having—a man cannot give unless he has it in the first place, and at the same time, he assuredly believes that his contingent future time is also provisioned adequately. A strong belief in completeness, in fullness, and in abundance is called for—an active IEE motor is, therefore, a necessity.

Essential Value Practices

Once a set of temporal value drivers conforming with universal ethics–abundance value set is identified, we need to see how they are blended into man's objective personality and reflect in everyday conducts of his life, see Figure 5.2.

Managing Surprises!

There are no guarantees steering one through the slippery slopes of scarcity—the passage to lofty planes of abundance could certainly be full of surprises. However, these surprises are well-nigh caused and created by man himself—no one else. The thought streams in mind travel even faster than light; therefore, expectations stem and roll much quicker than the result of actions—this is the keynote. So, surprises could just naturally happen—and man could do well to provision and provide for them. But, this is quite contrary to the stance of man on the ground who likes and accepts every single color as long as it is black! This is the most the contemporary mind could go in terms of managing surprises! This needs to be addressed!

Meditating on the Go!

Although Buddha sat in meditation under an exclusive tree, most of us need not separate life and meditation in such uncompromising manners, and instead, we could simply try to bring meditation itself to moments

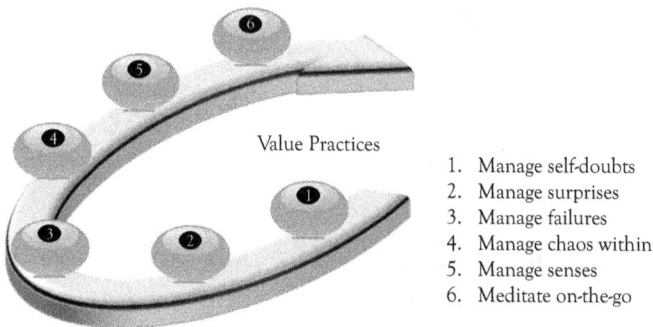

Value Practices

1. Manage self-doubts
2. Manage surprises
3. Manage failures
4. Manage chaos within
5. Manage senses
6. Meditate on-the-go

The value practices to sensitize the business actor
in order to establish connect with
ethics–abundance dimension of her existence.

Figure 5.2 The value practices

of our everyday life. In fact, that is what Buddha preached to his disciples after his enlightenment through meditation. As soon as man realizes that in every moment of his finite lifetime he has sourced from the abundance of infinite cosmic energy on the basis of a forthright cause–effect tribulation, he will naturally be disposed to love each and every moment of his life and enjoy them thoroughly as moments of truth. Man will have peace and joy in every stretch of his living—this is meditation happening inside him. No one could "do" meditation—it must happen upon her! It is not like a possession that could be acquired to feel good about it. In meditation, there is nothing except the moment—everything else is indispensably dropped altogether. It simply chaperons man to a state of inner stillness—*speaking* silence, as we borrow the term from Hartmut Rosa—in which he is neither hounded by desires nor tormented by fears—thereby sustained, connected with collective consciousness—a state of fullness (abundance), beyond the emptiness (scarcity).

It is, however, difficult for someone to simply drop everything, especially for something she has no idea about. This is when the IEE motor could be primed to explore *evolution through involution*. In the modern age of *Google search*, man has become used to knowing his destinations well in advance—but here man is unlikely to know where he is headed—this is little adventurous and must, therefore, be explored going beyond the security of his comfort zone. It is not possible to know it in advance—because once it is known, it is done—what else is there to know! A man is said to be in the state of freedom only when his individualistic ideas pertaining to his identity and associations in the phenomenal world are completely dissolved. The PPF and IEE motors must, therefore, be fully functional for mediation on the go!

Managing Senses!

The only way man could experience the phenomenal world is through his sense organs. All his experience could come only through his senses. Mind, as we argued, is either in the realm of no-more-valid past or in the puzzling not-yet-valid ambit of future—both being unreal should at best be left to fend for themselves. Instead, man should get in touch with his bio-gaia reality, and bypassing the mind, connect straight with abundance consciousness to realize his collective existence. In other words, man's experience in the awareness of collective consciousness alone could ensure his conclusive growth. Therefore, the sensitivity and awareness of man must be honed assiduously—his bio-gaia system must be reconditioned and cleansed of amassed habits that covertly caused the insensitivity and unspontaneity in his personality—and allowed his senses to age beyond dotage.

Managing Failures and Sufferings Within!

As a matter of fact, failure apes the vulnerability of man—otherwise, he could remain blind to it all throughout his life. It shows to him something to get out of and not remain with any longer. Whatever the failure, it is the man's personal problem and not anyone else's. Therefore, the first step is to take its full responsibility, and only then could he realize that the problem was within him and not anywhere else. Again, it requires a lot of self-convincing to accept that the suffering is originating from inside him and not from outside. It underscores what has been learned so far and what needs to be re-learned. However, the scarcity-prone mind, notwithstanding his misery, labels it an unfulfilled desire. It is only after years of pain and misery that man could realize he was possibly wrong—and this is exactly when he could possibly be right as the learning could then ensue. Peace is then restored in him as the inward campaign begins and the silence of abundance is plugged in—peace could be found only beyond the mind in collective consciousness. Failure is an indication from life that there is something that has to be amended—this must be understood, accepted and simply be mended!

Managing Chaos Within!

Life has a plan for humanity, and everyone is intrinsically included in it. It is also important to appreciate that there is no discriminating plan exclusive for any emblematic individual. Therefore, until man plugs into life without any exclusive exclusivity, he could remain insecure and fragile. Solo run with the objective ACE and CRR motor could turn out wobbling. And, each time, life could shock him, a new theory could be invented to shield the idea that life has some specific reason and some special purpose for him. And, even if there were to be one such concealed idea for him in the cosmos, it could never be known to him anyway—how could one fathom aggregate through fragments? At best, the individual could attempt to be inclusive in the cosmic collectiveness itself, and once it is be-chanced so, he could cease to see himself as someone special and stop making any exclusive sense out of his life. Once the whole is accepted within the abundance of collective consciousness, chaos vanishes, and conditioned rationality is bypassed.

Managing Self-Doubts!

Only doubts could connect man to collective consciousness, nothing else. Doubts appear only in the mind, and even the cause behind such doubts is assigned by the same mind, albeit to something outside of his individual self. The fact, however, is otherwise. The outside world is what it is for one and for all, without prejudice or bias toward any individual being. Doubt is an individual undertaking having its source within the individual self. And, to manage it, therefore, man must face the inside in him and not to the outside of him and then work on it. Some risk is to be taken to be with the situation until doubt is cleared and an authentic answer is gotten. It is only life—the uncaused collective consciousness that is beyond any reason—that could explain the doubts, the creations of mind. It is the collective mind that has caused the individual mind and its personal doubts—not the other way around. A happy mind has no questions—questions come from a problematic state of mind. Only a unclouded mind inquires, explores, and discovers—through self-caechization, so to say!

Practice! Practice! Practice!

Without a pertinent process and fitting method, it is not possible to reach the right place. However, the idea of right could be as wrong as the abyss of individual centricity of the right. In fact, those who are sure, they are intelligent—meaning they have even more deep-seated intransient beliefs and therefore need even more practice—the greater is man's intelligence, more internal is his individual sense and the idea of himself being a unique and atypical entity. It is not possible to reach the third step unless the first and second steps are completed. At the third step, however, the man could still believe that the first step was unnecessary—but to gain this belief itself—taking the first two steps were necessary. At the end of the process, however, man in all likelihood should realize the necessity of all the steps he took on. To arrive somewhere, man must walk himself. To enjoy life, man must explore the process himself—from A to Z on his own—and experience it all by himself. It should also be borne in mind that a particular practice is for a particular stage and therefore must be rejected altogether to move to another practice at different stage of process in amelioration. The central idea is that man himself should not, at any time, become the practice per se. Problem with the mind is that it clings to whatever it is in game with and that is the faux pas.

Value Spurs and Deployment Framework

Let us now get down to discuss the inducements to value assimilation in man and how these values could be deployed in his everyday work life, see Figure 5.3.

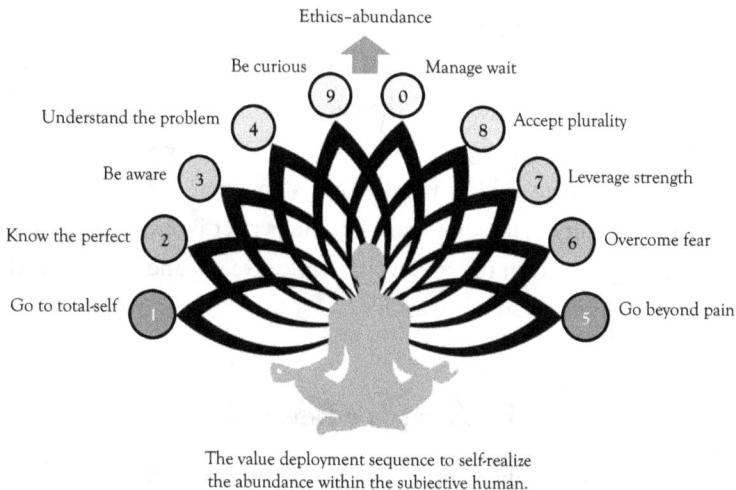

Ethics–abundance

Be curious   Manage wait
9   0

Understand the problem   4   8   Accept plurality

Be aware   3   7   Leverage strength

Know the perfect   2   6   Overcome fear

Go to total-self   1   5   Go beyond pain

The value deployment sequence to self-realize
the abundance within the subjective human.

Figure 5.3 Value spurs and deployment

Get to Total Self

Man suffers largely because he has not realized his collective self. He is in pain because he is refusing to accept an erring part of himself. An individualistic sorority has already entered inside his mind and made home out there. In fact, this is the emblematic reason he needs to fight that sorority within in the first place! Because it has already entered him, and he does not like it! Otherwise, there was no need to fight, and he should have just left the scene scrupulously.

Know the Perfect

Ironically, it is onerous upon man to accept that he is perfect and everything that he is trying to prove himself to be as perfect is for the most part meaningless—and in all likelihood, he is already positioned where he is trying to position himself in futurity. The distance between what he is and what he wants to be is sentient only in his mind—the gap is altogether there and nowhere else. Mistakenly, he is struggling forever to become someone else—just imagine the fight that is going on within him! Fancy a cat trying to fly, or a pigeon trying to swim! He continues to try thinking that he could be perfect one fine day. In fact, it is this idea of perfection that makes his life dispiriting. He cannot do a single thing that does not take him from somewhere to somewhere else. He works reservedly in order to become "perfect." However, in truth, he is already perfect—as perfect as he thinks he is. He is unhappy only because he is fighting with himself, and then, the entire world appears to be fighting with him because he is fighting within him. Objective self of the man is created only by his subjective self. This is how man is designed (recall the five personality planes, Figure 1.1). The perfect is already within the man awaiting his return to his very own collective self and self-realize the abundance within his subjective self!

Be Aware or Beware!

To realize the abundance within, the first thing that man must do is become aware of himself. The connect with abundance consciousness cannot be established with an addled and blurred mind. Problems never get solved unless they are understood properly. Awareness is not a thinking process—thinking is just a judgmental simulation leading to more problems. Awareness happens, and it is to be experienced. It must be adopted as it cannot be adapted. It is beyond the mind–intellect entanglement, as mind knows only to emote, and intellect knows only to judge—whereas awareness simply sees and allows expression of man's true free will. Therefore, awareness cannot be controlled, as control itself is a mind function. It is only when man becomes subservient to his search for awareness, he is getting close to abundance. This is when his mind could get to let go!

Understand the Problem

Intellect and the embedded logic therein maintain just the structure of mind and its belief athenaeum. It cannot tender understanding, which is not about analyzing, thinking, or concluding—these are all functions of the mind. To understand, man must go beyond logic to awareness. Only awareness could develop understanding. And, when understanding is developed, a part of the mind is felled, and the energy used up in maintaining the structure of belief gets released. It frees the man from a belief, supported by the logic of his intelligence, and he gets back to natural expressions of unitive energies such as love, trust, fun, and the likes. He could then place himself in a situation where understanding could happen—it cannot be done forcefully. Once the man stops protecting his logic, understanding starts maturing.

Go Beyond Pain

The only thing that could transform a man is pain, nothing else. Pain cannot be analyzed. The purpose of pain is to obliterate a portion of the mind. And, like a needle, it punctures the bubble of idea or the belief concealed within the fissures of mind. So, the best response from man could be to allow pain to burst the bubble and let pain do whatever it wants to the mind. Pain could destroy only what must be destroyed, nothing else. Let the abundance of unitive life energy deal with the pain. Man could remain safe as long as he is beyond the clutches of the disorderly mind and connected with the inexhaustible and abundant source of existential energy. To go beyond mind, however, the man must go beyond all that is suppressed in it—every fictitious ideas, he is identified with, must go. And, only pain could help him do that.

Overcome Fear

Oddly enough, beliefs alone shelter fear in a man's mind. Beliefs are by the mind and solely for the mind—they do not serve any other cause or purpose. Cause of fear cannot serve its own cause of analyzing it and over-coming it! All in all, the very belief must therefore be dropped—the *idea of fear* that is held up in the roughcast of mind. Fear comes only when there is some threat to the ideas or beliefs corrugated in the mind. Any thought that runs through mind is part of a belief system—fear is part of man's that belief system. It works on a self-fulfilling presage—thoughts support beliefs, and in turn, beliefs set up more thoughts. The more a man identifies with individual self, much added is the fear of losing that identity. A bed of fire could be seen as a bed of flowers as well only if the belief is dropped that the fire must burn. Fear simply takes away the freedom of a man. Therefore, if there is fear, there is also an opportunity to drop a belief.

Leverage the Unmitigated Strength

Only an indisposed mind could be disposed to bugs and bugbear. The number of bugs in the mind is indicative of its weakness. It is well suited to the mind to boast of its strength only from the fortification of its comfort zone. The comfort zone is the citadel of beliefs that mind has contrived to position itself in a factitious strong stead. It has nothing to do with the unmitigated strength of man, which exudes only from his ever-been being—his unitive collective consciousness. These beliefs pro-vide a mistaken sense of being in control for the mind. On the contrary, mind could hardly control anything, including even its own mind-self. True strength comes from his abundance self which has no conditions—no pretentions! It does not require any idea of external strength to sup-port it—it is self-supported and self-sustained. But, ironically, the most insecure and unreliable relationship a man has is with his very own self-secured and ever-reliable abundance consciousness—the stomping ground of his authentic strength!

Accept Plurality

The only difference between a man and the other is the extent of disparate degree of acceptance in them. What one feels, all others might as well feel—except that someone could accepts it completely without fight against his feelings, while the other may not. The very *acceptance* helps the mind to remain calm and unaffected even in the midst of the inner fight that is perpetuating within it. Acceptance brings awareness as well—and just this awareness could help mind to overcome even the anger suppressed within it. It could allow the mind to feel the emotions completely without any labels attached to it—that is the power of acceptance. An un-accepting mind could continue to be angry even when the situations around have changed and the prompts for anger have disappeared—fight against the anger continues within it as it ever was. Similarly, acceptance could also support the mind to overcome depression. Like happiness, anger and depression are simply natural emotions—and once they are accepted, mind of its own is capable of dealing with them straight out. Everything could become light-hearted with unconditional acceptance. This is the balanced mind in which the past and future are altogether subsumed in present—the PPF motor is wholly active.

Be Curious, Not Serious!

It could be interesting to observe that some of the most respected men in our midst appear most serious for reasons only best known to them! While this is not intended to be any left-handed complement to those respected beings, fact remains that the very purpose of life—to be happy, is forgotten completely by these ponderous men. Ironical as it is—being celebrative and satisfied is invariably linked to being unproductive. Let us, therefore, try and understand what we mean by celebration. Firstly, it is certainly not an escape from misery. Even pleasure for man is ugly if it is to escape from his pains. Natural joy cannot have hangover.

On the contrary, it must plant a smile on the face to blossom. Work is joy for only those who are joyous already—otherwise, it is either misery or an escape from it—and in both ways, it is painful. Work has no richness contained in it—it is the man who could infuse abundance into it and make it more meaningful for all those impacted by his work. This is true job enrichment that management gurus talk about. We tend to look for some cause to get something—even to experience joy. However, cause is just an inert encumbrance that could deliver pain as well in some different configuration. Enduring joy is causeless—and seeks no reason. Work should, therefore, be for its own sake. For this, the man must bypass the mind–intellect structure and connect straight with the primary source of joy—his collective consciousness. The ethical man works not seriously but curiously with open and alert mind to experience joy in the collective human flourish. The usual defense offered for his serious demeanor is the mound of responsibilities befallen on his shoulders. But, the fact remains that he has willingly taken up these responsibilities and therefore cannot complain about them anymore. Once the responsibility is taken, it must be acted upon with joy—or it must be repudiated altogether from life—everything man has in his life is because of his own choice!

Manage the Wait

Wait or patience should not be mistaken with resignation—while resignation is consuming and withering, patience is dynamic and buoyant. Wait by its essential characteristic is inestimable—it therefore, has to be forever. When something completely unknown has to be explored, the attribute of waiting must be necessarily vested by the mind. More so, when the mysterious abundance consciousness is to be approached. Mind tends to "time" even time, but man must go beyond the mind-bounded time to the realm of timeless time, where time ceases to have any external-to-it reference of measure. Therefore, hurry must be buried right away if the goal is the superordinate goal—the one without any ordinates. There cannot be a play of rush in the expedition to collective consciousness. The high heap of beliefs gathered in the mind over a long period of man's life must dissolve, and mind should be made open to course its way through unchartered waters—it requires an inestimable time for that. Exploring truth is an uncertain journey—and the mind must learn to live with uncertainty. In the alleys to abundance, there is certainly no room for security—although its sure and secure when man is there. Therefore, each doubt defended by the mind must be brought into open and be faced—that shows the mind where it is lacking—man must be aware of them, rather than seeking answers for each one of them all the time. Answer-seeking tends to cease the flow of mind further into onward movement—and cast the mind in the same place. So, the questioning must be dropped—but not the questions per se! Trust and patience will ultimately deliver what they must! There is no need to hurry or worry for every practical detail to be foreseen and resolved in advance before taking each step forward. If the direction of the track is correct to begin with, the rest of it will eventually fall in place sooner or later.

And Be Free!

The indeterminate part of freedom is that no one could be free when he wants to be free—freedom cannot come to anyone simply because he is trying to accrue it. Being free from something acknowledges its existence in the first place. And, trying to do so is called *running away* from it—it is *escaping* and not *freedom*. A free man is free already—now and always. He was never bonded—not even to the idea of being free. On the contrary, he is free even to be bonded at his own will. For him, illusion is no longer delusion, as he knows it is illusion and he could get in and out of it at his own discretion—that is the extent of his freedom! Freedom comes from abundance—it is, therefore, uncaused and complete—never partial. In true sense, freedom has no degrees attached to it. It is there in whole nine yards, or it is not there even a bit. It is not dependent on anything or anyone. A free man is free everywhere—at all times. It has its own adequacy embedded into it. The free was always free!

The Key Takeaway

It is only during times of sudden and swift change that the need for keeping in touch with basics and fundamentals assumes even greater significance. It must be clearly understood—the difference between a *system failure* and *ethics value failure.* Only flowing water is pure spring, not stagnant water. In order to achieve long-term resilience through ethical anchorage, we must consider pouring as much energy into sensitizing the mind to ethical values, as it is being done in modern times to stimulate emblematic oddities. This overarching and long-term vision should, therefore, become the constant and unfailing yardstick for all decisions and actions in all domains of human life. Man's understanding of ethics and values has become lopsided. The collective human is missed out completely for the individual man. The existential purpose of man is to re-establish his connect with the human within, and this is dependent upon the strength of his ethical moorings and ethics–value predisposition. Any progress or growth accompanied by value insouciance achieved in a climate of ethical vacuity cannot be sustained for long.

PART II

Prescription

CHAPTER 6

Metric for Growth Versus Framework for Longevity

Business Ethics or Ethics in Business

With man at the fulcrum, business is no doubt an institutionalized version of individual or group of individuals. Nevertheless, business ethics, as a term is often used by businesses, seems to sanction a set of economic and commercial activities to pass off as ethical, even though from the collective human perspective, they may not. The legitimate test of ethics in business, however, lies in the capacity of a business decision or activity to include in it the element of human flourish in a sustainable and righteous way in the widest possible collective and ubiquitous sense. The presumptuous corporate mission assertion must be questioned from the viewpoint of its suitability and relevance in the context of overall sustainability of the bio-gaia system and for the simple reason that unless business ethics is established in a framework of ethics in business, which is congruent with the ubiquitous ethical dimension of the human–nature interrelationship, it will continue to provide lopsided justifications to business decisions. It might not be prudent for the long-term sustenance and advancement of the business. There is an inescapable cause-and-effect link between all-embracing sustainability of human gaia system and ethical-ity.

Quantification and Ethics in Business

There is a bottom-line quantification syndrome in businesses that often confronts even basic and preliminary steps being taken toward ethics in business. And, the hackneyed dilemma of the business analyst, in this context, relates to the likelihood of accruing tangible results from these efforts in *business in ethics* and any adverse impact that could cumulate in

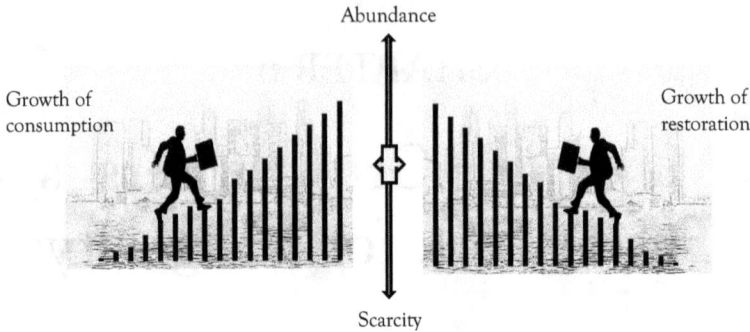

The key element of the longevity framework is consumption–restoration
balance for the sustainability of bio-gaia system.

Figure 6.1 Balancing growth and longevity

the bottom-line if such efforts are not taken up first-off. These posers could
be portended impetuously or in a roundabout way. However, the business
think-tank invariably ducks and side-steps to the next item on the strategic
agenda of the debate. And, questions that remain routinely unanswered
are: how would it be possible to sustain the business system without sustenance of the all-inclusive human gaia system and should business ethics
be vindicated by the letter of business economy or the spirit of business
comport? We are, therefore, as always, on the crossroad where we stand
to miss the expansive human viewpoint that ethics is its own vindication.
Ethics–abundance is uncaused and self-sustained and therefore begs no
apology or justification. Economic growth cannot be sustained unless a
commensurate growth of restoration of the bio-gaia system is ensured. It
is a subjective excellence that spurs objective excellence at both individual
and business levels, and not the other way round. Therefore, ethics cannot
be quantifiably explicated, see Figure 6.1.

Roots of Ethical Capability

As we discussed, ethics belongs to a world beyond the mind–intellect
system. Therefore, there is no room for pretentious emotions or chichi
feelings or the manipulative rationality here. As soon as it is subjected to
any externalized debate or discussion and attempted to grasp it through
the language of economics and commerce, it could become mystifying
and confusing and become a real hurdle to proceed further to make sense

of it. Therefore, unless such attempts to comprehend ethics–abundance incorporate a certain ability to still one's mind as against tilling it, the desired purpose could be found lacking. Mind must be free of objective entropy and economic–commercial hara-kiri to enter the domain of ethics–abundance. One simply cannot decide whether the thing decided is good or bad. The de facto value of an economic–commercial activity is dependent on its applicability in the pervasive human–nature framework. So, the judgment of value cannot be intellectual in origin, and intellect by itself is not the source of all actions. The motives of an action are necessarily the desires concealed in man's mind. The firm ground of ethicality has to ultimately to rest upon well-developed instinctive probity based on a thoroughly groomed and balanced mind.

Hierarchy: The Structure for Longevity

Flat organization is often a favorite topic of discussion in the corridors of administration. A certain measure of rhetoric often raised among several management savants is that hierarchy in business organizations is a factor inhibiting creative and effective performance of its members. They also allege that hierarchy obstructs communication channels and even vitiates contact between business actors. Furthermore, hierarchy is also being labeled as *cost to be looked into*—and the first action item for the next round of ensuing cost-cutting measures to improve the bottom-line results. At times, hierarchy is being associated with even infructuous absolutism. Cognitive values such as equality, autonomy, self-esteem, and the likes also implore the efficacy and validity of organizational hierarchy.

A purely economic–commercial view of hierarchy, however, ignores the more subtle business longevity aspects of interpersonal relationship between business actors. Although it could be valid that over a period of time, hierarchy has developed into a sort of antiquated structure, but given a rightful ethics–abundance orientation, it must be able to more than offset all such genuine or alleged encumbrances convincingly. It could hardly be discounted that each one of the actors in business setting is combined in an interpersonal relationship in which someone is superior to, subordinate to, or equal to another. But, this is how an actor's family life is structured—and a human's aggregate relationship is structured all through her lifetime! And, therefore, like familial hierarchy, organizational hierarchy should also continue to deliver stability and balance to the business structure—and at the same time, provide the ethics–abundance pressures upon business actors to adhere to collective values and superordinate goals necessary to harmonize illimitable and engaging management without clamor or topsy-turvies.

Hierarchy also builds a mentorship structure within the day-to-day milieu of an actor's work life. Equality cannot be equated with the *lowest common denominator*. On the contrary, it should raise low-lingering individualistic minds to higher and stronger collective tenets of abundance consciousness, where the higher–lower levels are just to ensure that the spring of life is gushing through across all planes in the business architecture. Hierarchy, thus, imposes a psychological covenant on leader actors to strive for higher standards of ethical conduct and at the same time acts as an effective brake against heedless egocentricity in interpersonal relationship among the follower actors federated otherwise in a flat organizational structure. Operating at a higher level of ethics–abundance consciousness also serves at times, a mean to resolve day-to-day inter-functional conflicts by way of going beyond the considerations of economics–commerce. Hierarchy also ensures patience and discipline among the various business actors in the organization. In effect, hierarchy with emollients like forgiveness, patience, care, support, humility, loyalty and so on set up the *veritable network* of inter-related business actors within the organization. The crucial cog in a business longevity framework therefore, is the structure of the leader–follower relationship within the organization—economic growth in business builds and thrives on the strength of this relationship. The basic manifesto of the leader–follower relationship in the organization could, therefore, be comprehended thus:

1. The underlying strength of the organization structure builds bottoms up. Therefore, stability and durability of business longevity framework rests to a great extent on combining obedience with self-respect on the part of follower actor.
2. The business could achieve substantive excellence only along the distinctive character of the leader–follower relationship embodied in everyday work interactions, practices, systems, and the like to hold

the psyche of business actors unified in the hierarchical structure at a synchronous wavelength.

3. Through sustained efforts and practice, a distinctive business character is to be built in which all individual-centric appetence gets dissolved with no big role to be played by the mind or intellect.

4. An abundance-oriented mind combined with passion for collective human is the essential authority of a leader in this relationship.

5. At the initial stages of this culture building exercise, democratic principles of decision making could also be held in latency. Such principles could be plugged in later, when, with better spread of such culture, members could recoil from individual-centric proclivities for the collective good. Until such time, the organization could run by way of *enlightened dictatorship,* the formulate we borrow from the book, *Moments of Truth* (1985), by Jan Carlzon, former CEO of SAS Group—we ascribe enlightened dictatorship to abundance-oriented leadership in this context. Logic and emotions could scarcely comprehend the blend of autocracy-democracy that is needed to build the organizational structure and express collective passion and compassion. To model compassion, the mind must abandon its scarcity machination and go beyond petty emotions and rudiment rationales to collective abundance.

6. To gain insight and true perspective into knotty management problems, systematic deceleration and a *still* mind are essential—without going beyond the mind, no collective vision is possible.

7. Obedience and allegiance from follower actors must be commanded based on impeccable integrity, rather than bargains of convenience on the part of the leader actor.

8. Leadership is not about the calculus of give-and-take or quid pro quos of performance against rewards—rather, the follower actors must be kept alive by the leader actor to a vision that transcends beyond their narrow individual sense.

9. Compassion, discipline, forbearance—much needed to develop the business longevity framework are deceptively simple codes, and yet, they require a rigorous and sustained effort to live by.

The essential spirit of hierarchy is that the senior actor is encouraged to defer, even deny her own claims and entitlements in favor of the junior actor—it is the spirit of caring, obligation, and sacrifice by former to the latter—and only then, in return, is the junior actor expected to offer her loyalty, support, and obedience to the senior actor. Value inertia, developed through the gradient inseparably embodied in hierarchy, could interconnect all business actors in keeping with the hierarchical structure of cosmic design itself. This is certainly not a dependency structure, rather it is an attempt to transform the individual actors' consciousness by seeking to relate to their respective senior actors in harmony with the aboriginal and venerable caring framework of human relationship—the leader–follower hierarchy.

Longevity and the Four-Goal System

The business longevity framework for sustained human development must be based on ideals and not on mere ideologies. A business is human first and economics–commerce later. It is the latter that is to serve the former, and not the other way around. Therefore, businesses as the superstructure of human aspiration cannot escape the engagement with ideals, just as the individual actor contemplating her total development cannot choose to remain insulated from ethical probity. The answer to complexity mushrooming out of a scarcity mind is simply its opposite—the simplicity radiating out from the abundance mind. The subjective–objective motors, as we discussed, need to be focused uprightly on a four-goal system to drive business agenda for the growth of business actors in collective consciousness toward total human excellence:

1. Collective prosperity—economical–commercial success through the ACE motor
2. Collective well-being—physical–emotional wholeness through the CRR motor
3. Collective present—idolize–nourish the unified present through the PPF motor
4. Collective self—total freedom from individual self through the IEE motor

The existential goals of material, physical, and emotional well-being are integrated into the model within the bounds of ethical propriety and total freedom—the ultimate ascendancy of the business actor from an individual self into the realm of collective self. Collective consciousness, the uncaused cause of material manifestation, crystallizes the universal infinite energy into finite matter, mind, and lifetime. The goal of business actors, above everything else, is to seize this dynamic and realize their original state of collective consciousness. This is the longevity of causeless sustenance in which the business no longer exists for a cause, but matures as cause of well-being of the collective actor in business.

Growth Metric and Longevity Framework

The scarcity maxim as well as the abundance principle must be inferred with a degree of abundant caution, as the practical consequences of these two opposite principles could err upon the ethical alignment of business actors and the longevity of business in the overall sustainability of the bio-gaia system in radically different ways. The scarcity-led temper of business actors coupled with the metrics-n-measure criterion of business growth could easily push the business into the vicinity of a bottomless pit. On the other hand, the immeasurable abundance-led quintessential temper has perpetually preserved and sustained the bio-gaia system through the infinites of time, only to be exploited and brought close to collapse by the metrics-driven business enlargements and accessions. In a way, therefore, both scarcity and abundance are exploited—if scarcity is the dominant perspective, then conservation should go naturally with it, and if abundance is the prime driver of business decisions, then sustenance of bio-gaia existence in collective consciousness must be the all-pervading business theme—this is the marrow.

Of course, the idea of scarcity and managing metrices within such constrictions delivers a sense of achievement and tangibility to business actors—a reward for the labor, so to say. But, typically, tangibility has short tenure, and it alters and falters unabashedly with uncontrolled greed–speed acceleration as we see. If the abundance principle could define a business entity more wholesomely, then its precepts should, of course, be embraced straight way as a guide in everyday conduct of the business actors with a temporal–cultural fine-tuning appropriately accommodated. The ethics–abundance basis of human peace and flourish

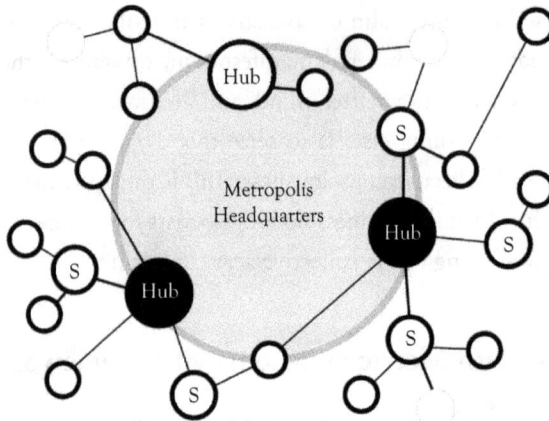

Hub and spoke rural BPO model to expand operations
deeper into rural habitations. The spokes (S) manage the
delivery centers in the near vicinity.

Figure 6.2 The hub and spoke model for rural BPO

is another casualty of objective metric-ism. Subjective custodian-ism, by
contrast, seems to be ethically sounder both in the sphere of actor–actor
relationship and that of actor–nature relationship, as ethically sound
actions exude necessarily from the sense of collective-ness. This is where
subjective custodian-ism could score over objectivity metric-ism.

The model of localized, decentralized, and self-contained cooperative economy readily captures the spirit of subjective custodian-ism.
As against developing huge castles of infrastructure and mobilizing masses
of women and men to congregate at the hub of business's metropolitan
headquarters, a Chennai-based BPO company experimented and success-
fully established a decentralized hub and spoke rural BPO operation in
the 1990s, see Figure 6.2.

In this disparate *hub and spoke operations model* for global delivery
of BPO services, local rural women and men trained by the firm joined
the rural local spoke of service delivery managed by a rural local entre-
preneur actor. The overall operation not only delivered consistent and
high-quality output at a much lower operating cost, but also the high
comradeship among the unit actors seen reflected in terms of exception-
ally low employee absenteeism and remarkably high customer satisfaction

index. This was a simple and predictable system unlike comparable complex and on-the-edge operation systems. While the latter does collapse under its own weight, the former appeared more nimble, flexible, predictable, consistent, and self-measured. The young and energetic rural business actors in service delivery were seen most comfortable in their natty small groups—the village–town is the association, which is found so perfectly natural to this human trait. And, because it is less crowded with complex man-made constraints, holism as a culture always has a better chance to flourish even going forward—for work ethics to survive, time and space must be compatible with man in the cosmic energy–matter–time disposition. Man must, therefore, stay local, and it is his consciousness that has to become thoroughly universal and include the wholistic bio-gaia existence for business longevity, which is nothing but an economic system to serve the collective human. The metrics-n-measure and greed–speed driven global-ism should be replaced with a self-contained and holistically contented local-ism for ethics–abundance to reveal its legitimate authority.

Dignity in Local and Flourish in Universal

To a certain degree, insecurity exists in all humans, but culture and education are designed to counter this scarcity-fueled insecurity and uncover the hitherto concealed subjective personality of humans, which is unitive, collective, and hence completely secured in the abundance consciousness. The ethics–abundance principle has inspired humans to be the social beings and evolve a way to keep their scarcity mind in check by developing a part of their being to abide by certain set of ethical principles and guidelines for their existence and survival in their small communities beyond the wayward and instant pleasure-seeking megalomania. Small communities also serve and act as reciprocal pressure groups to keep the flock on track along some basic ethical norms and temporally binding ethical practices. They also allow humans to foresee conflicts within a longer-lasting relationship with fellow humans as well as the surrounding ecology. The idea of developing small and local community groups helps establish an economic environment where the dignity threshold needs of the business actor—so necessary for her consummate flourish—could also be met. When humans could build capabilities to develop themselves and their communities to achieve higher levels of well-being, they do create conditions for such flourishing. Every human has a set of individual needs—physical, emotional, and social—in order to live a life in dignity. Only when the human dignity is supported, human flourish could be promoted.

Measure of the Immeasurable

The faculties of mind–intellect—like emotions, intelligence, or memory—are not autonomous but derive their significance from the uncaused collective consciousness or, we could also say, collective intelligence. The manifested measurable is caused by the uncaused immeasurable. The human frame enfolds an indestructible core of this collective intelligence, the source of perpetual knowledge, and mind usually remains disconnected from this all-inclusive intelligence and wisdom due to the thick layer of unfulfilled desires and yet continues to perform its phenomenal machinations—but the individual self then misses the guidance of the collective self. Therefore, all actions by the business actor gravitate more toward problem creation rather than prevention, prompting an increase in ethical entropy. The manipulative individual mind crowded with numbers, checklists, schedules, analytics, and so on, therefore, loses its communion with the straightforward collective mind.

The leader actor, therefore, must come to terms with the realization that the finite-fragmented human intelligence or reason cannot grasp the infinite collective intelligence. An auxiliary subset cannot hold the necessary total set within it. Once such awakening is stirred, the individual actor, with tools of reason, logic, and measurement begins to manifest constructive and creative powers of progressively greater intuitive certitude. The small and local community work groups structure then helps the leader actor to see the power of immeasurable collective intelligence and allows her to nurture it in furtherance of the holistic growth of follower actors engaged in such enterprise.

The Key Takeaway

Measurements, rules, and regulations are objective and therefore confine to the dominion and the period in time. Ethics–abundance is an immeasurable subjective code—therefore, it is perennial and beyond time. Collective consciousness, the abode of all-embracing ethics–abundance code, is the uncaused source of all material—therefore, it is beyond any sort of material need or gain and yet engaged in incessant work. This is the personality of collective actor—the perpetual role model in the performance of all-inclusive collaborative agenda is beyond individual self-ness and measures of any economic objective. This *perpetuity* and *individual selfless-ness* of the collective actor in the infinite scheme of expansive work provide the much-needed inspiration for stability and sanctity to all her local cooperative endeavors. The idea of longevity is, therefore, beyond the feeling-level full-ness of emotional mind or the measurement metrics construct of the rational mind. Without entirely ruling out the relevance of measures and internal controls to support the business conduct conforming to dominion codes, the theme of longevity extends this indispensable yet fragile economic frame and reaches out to the ultimate irrefutable foundation of ethics–abundance and the sense of identity with the collective self. It is important to understand the collectivity—the collective objectives—the superordinate goal.

The man-in-human is a profound paradox—without the individual self as nucleus, no individual personality could begin to form, and yet, when this initial indispensable and formative function of the individual self is established, it turns to entwine an exclusive macrocosm altogether for its own self. The entire hierarchy of natural and complimentary relationship with other selves, thus, suffers the constant threat of breach and burst. It becomes imperative for all human development processes to create within itself a framework for cooperative collaborative working and a framework for longevity.

CHAPTER 7

Motivating Exclusivity Versus Inspiring Inclusivity

Every part of the human body has a different role, and it is readily accepted as part of the whole body. However, the same business actor finds it painfully difficult to accept fellow actors in a four-member team in her own workplace! Subjective unity gets so easily replaced with objective differentiation! Ethics–abundance inspired culture-building within a business will certainly demand a well-sanitized, vibrant, expressive, and enlivening philosophy as well as firm obedience to details for its translation into thought and action. From the hoisted rostrum of abundance consciousness alone, the business actor could get to her teeming reflection and see herself in relation to others in the circumambient fraternity.

Inclusivity: Back to the Roots

In the context of a business organization, there are three levels of consciousness: individual self, group self, and collective self. Ethics–abundance is an increasing function of these ascending levels of consciousness. The primary characteristics of particularly the individual self-level consciousness are:

- Primary motivation in self-expediency and self-preference
- Basic agenda is self-eminence through differentiation and self-ascendancy through self-prevalence
- Emotional orientation is self-gratification
- Intellectual learning is unyielding and hype-amenable
- Dignity is splashing but emotionally petty

- Relationship goal is to establish self-rights or self-authority and bonding is for bondage
- Behavioral unfolding is centrifugal, vulnerable, and solicitous
- Success is maximum and self-exhilaration is mistaken as joy

In the entire bio-gaia system, only humans possess a unique ability to connect with the all-inclusive abundance consciousness. Rest on the other side of the human–nature schema exists and survives only in the restraints of the finite scarcity consciousness. There is no ethics–abundance involved when a carnivorous predatory subjugates the other for food. Even for coronaviruses, it is hardly an ethics–abundance issue when they enter and torment a sane and stainless human body. The ethics–abundance question is germane only for humans because they alone possess the contemplative abundance consciousness. Humans alone possess the idea of inclusivity in the abundance of collective consciousness. For humans, scarcity is unnatural to their being-ness. The individual self in reality is indivisible—it cannot be divided or disconnected from its root, the collective self. The individuality no doubt serves her identity—divisible or indivisible, fractional or complete, exclusive or inclusive—it is the inquiry that remains!

Motivating the Individual or Inspiring the Collective!

The design of motivation is, therefore, very spastic—if an individual actor could be motivated, she could be demotivated as well once the factors of motivation are rumpled. Instead, if the same actor is inspired, then the energy augmentation within her is invariable, immutable, and enduring. Motivation could as well appear in the guise of a contagion business environment, one in which unethical means force-push its actors much against their willingness toward individual centricity and short-term causatum. But, the short term cannot ignore the long term for long, and individuality cannot ignore collectivity ad infinitum. The dubious agenda of motivation must be seen through, and the victim aspect of the duplicitous ethical existence in self-centeredness must be exposed. The business actor must safely guard against such infections even if it were not her doing. The actor in business must discover the collective human within her who could inspire her to inclusivity and not fall prey to the machinations of motivation stratagem that promote such abject exclusivity. The master human cannot be a gudgeon-man. Therefore, the only expedient and prudent response to the question of exclusivity–inclusivity hubbub is to take charge and be inspired to cultivate collectivity so natural in humans and seek unshakable abode in the abundance of collective consciousness.

Individuality, however, is not the individualism. To be inclusive is to be a responsible individual in collective endeavors toward collective good. Both ethical degeneration and rejuvenation necessarily originate in and fluctuate around the individual values and ethical-ity flowing from collective values. To make a beginning, the business actor owes it to herself to nurture individual values as a mean to realize true inclusivity and complete alignment with collective consciousness. And this process, followed by more and more individual actors could go a long way in reducing the sallowness of business cultures in terms of values and pave the way for gradual subduing of unethical business exchanges, eventually raising the level of inclusivity in the all-around business environment.

Inspiring Leader, Uplifting Leadership

Leadership transpires when the leader inspires. In the collective consciousness, leadership revolves around the basic provisions of impartiality and non-exclusivity. However, impartiality is not the cold indifference or disinterest, but a wider all-embracing collective exertion of mind that could transcend the pettiness of misplaced loyalties and listless affections as well as personal distaste and discriminating discord. The collective consciousness for the follower actors relates to their lateral relationships constituting the foundation of sanction, collaboration, receptivity, proportioning, and so on. This calls for discipline founded in non-indulgence, temperance, and individual selflessness on the part of the leader actor. The follower actors, on their part, must exhibit through their conduct an invigorating bonding quality of assent to hierarchism, obedience, practice, and procedure in their everyday work relationship.

Leadership–Followership Character Amelioration

A surface behavior lends itself to easier measurement and statistical treatment. Therefore, *behavior* is typically considered a scientific construct—the term *behavioral science* is possibly the outcome of such postulate. On the other hand, *character* defies any such analytical treatment, so behavioral scientists tend to deny even a supine trunk with it. Although a business begins at the objective end of the human system, it must ultimately close-loop its progression to the subjective end of the human system at some point for its vitality. Steven Covey has also emphasized the difference between *character ethic* and *personality ethic* in his book, *Principle-Centered Leadership (1989)*. Therefore, character cannot be relegated to the confines of so-called *personal precinct,* as done so often by management theorists and practitioners alike. But, we are dauntlessly convinced that unless a leader actor as a human being could inspire her own self to the lofty dignity established in a meritorious character in widest possible sense of the word, there is little chance for any qualified leadership in her. Job competence and knowledge are also necessary, but they by themselves are inadequate for leadership performance and observance.

However, leadership is a leader–follower consent—both are integral as well as indispensable to it. The character of the follower actor is, therefore, equally compelling, and for an inclusive leadership to be established in the business, it is entirely necessary to sensitize each one of the business actors to both leadership and followership character—an actor in business is both a leader to followers and a follower to leader. The follower actors must be educated to overcome self-centered-ness, pretensions, rebellion, restlessness, and so on, if at all seated in their subjective persona. The significance of this character fine-tuning cannot be lost in the unsettling din of individuality, exemption, immunity, self-determination, parity, and the like. While there are scores of plans and programs that perdure in the leadership development schema of businesses, the followership perspective is left to be dealt with, if at all, by the leaders or the followers themselves. But, fact remains that the quality of followership character within the business actor could alone build the quality of the leadership character in her and not the other way around—and bypassing the followership character amelioration to reshape the leadership character would, therefore, be no more than cosmetic.

Serial Leadership, Period Leader

The acceleration of pace of business life affects interpersonal relationships of business actors and also the relationship of individual actor with her workspace and work time. Hastening of business life alters both the intensity and magnitude of everyday action episodes she is engaged with. It also alters her experience of events created by way of such action episodes. The pace of business life, thus, not only transforms the way business actors do things, but also the way they are—their identities and the way they relate with their individual selves. In other words, the identity of the business actor is really a function of her relationship with the inter-mutual business environment, the relationship with time and with her fellow actors, as well as with her actions and the reciprocal experience thereof. And, therefore, her identity is reflected in her actions and all such relationships—both these aspects are, thus, interdependent. However, the identity per se of the business actor is dynamic—adjusting and amending with the accelerating pace of her business life and modifies her relationship with fellow actors and her own self as well as her way of being at all times.

The individual actor in the overall relationship structure of business actors is essentially bound by three roles—a leader, a follower, and a lateral associate. The intensity of business life impacts the individual actor's dispensation in all three roles in a reciprocal framework in which the past, present, and future of all other business actors are also inclusive and inter-connected in the role pattern. Therefore, the individual actor in a role is defined by *how she became it, what she was and could have been, and what she will be and wants to be.* In other words, her past is regularly reconstructed—at the same time her present is reinterpreted—and a remodified future is reprojected for her. And, the degree of inclusivity–exclusivity in the prevalent work culture shapes the individual and collective identity of the business actors. In some business cultures, this identity could be developed through past orientation, while in other, it could be shaped by expectations and plans for future. The present—encroached

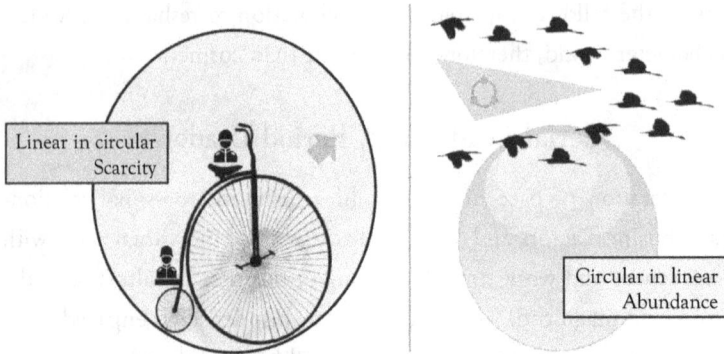

The myth of linearity is disproved by the flock of birds flying in circularity. Each bird is a leader and a follower at different point of time and advances linearly along a circular flight path. This is the idea of *serial leadership* and *period leader*.

Figure 7.1 Serial leadership and period leader

by the past and the future—is the new past–future-dominated present anyways, refer back Figure 3.4.

Thus, the leader actor cannot not be taken as a permanent leader for all action episodes and event times. In this scenario, the actor is not a leader, rather she performs as a leader for a particular event or episode. And, this ever-changing leader identity, which is dynamic in time and locus, is her new identity. The individual self, thus, collapses into a non-affirmative actor self that no longer identifies with any die cast roles and relationships. The leader in this inclusive frame of—every actor is a leader, follower, and associate—is to be visualized as a *period leader* in a *serial leadership*. A leader is not the one sitting on a high pedestal carrying the follower flock along on her back, but a member of the leadership configuration in which different actors, based on the nature of events and episodes, alternate in a serial leadership architecture as period leader along with her fellow actors, see Figure 7.1.

This is the inclusive leadership framework in which the individual and collective identity of the actor could naturally synchronize with the pace of business. In a distinct possibility, the leader actor could also assume the role of a teacher—which also implies playing the student—on alternate basis. Thus, the individual actor could be spurred to internalize and project higher ethical values more deeply and genuinely than if the job were delegated to other offline programs and initiatives.

The teaching process could also provide a strong moral drive to practice what is preached, when the period leader assumes the role of period mentor as well. As all behavioral changes are preceded by a commiserate thought change, the learn-cum-teach methodology of serial leadership could be the head start for the transformation process of leader actor as well as the business as a whole.

The Key Takeaway: Inclusive Work Structure

Inclusivity as an acclimation and the perspective for everyday work performance implies a progressive enlargement of the subjective frame of business actors engaged in such action episodes. This, in fact, is the grounding philosophy for ethics–abundance in many of the cooperative businesses today. While the temporal codes, laws, systems, and designs are all necessary for the mundane administration of everyday business affairs, the underlying ethics–abundance tone must be meant for long-term efforts on the basis of a stable formation of inclusivity. The work structure, therefore, must be so designed that it could promote interpersonal ethics as well as ethics in business as a whole in an inclusive construct of the business itself.

It could be admissible here to discuss the case of an inclusive work structure that was introduced by us in two separate business entities at different time frames (2004 and 2011) and managed by two uniquely differentiated leadership styles and work cultures, see Figure 7.2.

In the de novo model of functional design, we call, *the Troika Work Structure,* there are four distinct troikas combined within the overall altered structure of business functions—the overall business troika. Three different sub-entities of the respective businesses performed their distinctive roles in an exclusive troika relationship frame. And, each one of the four troikas—based on their unique functional character—is interlinked with other troikas within the overall troika structure of the business to deliver efficient and comprehensive engagement experience to all the stakeholders in the business. The classical quality control function is redesigned to expand its vision to *total quality* (we will discuss total quality in the following pages) instead of a narrow focus on product–service quality. An inclusive expression phrasing such as *member support*

Production/
Delivery

TROIKA-1

Total
Quality

Member
support

TROIKA-4

TROIKA-2

TROIKA-3

Technology/
R&D

Commercial
analytics

Patron support/
Sales and Marketing

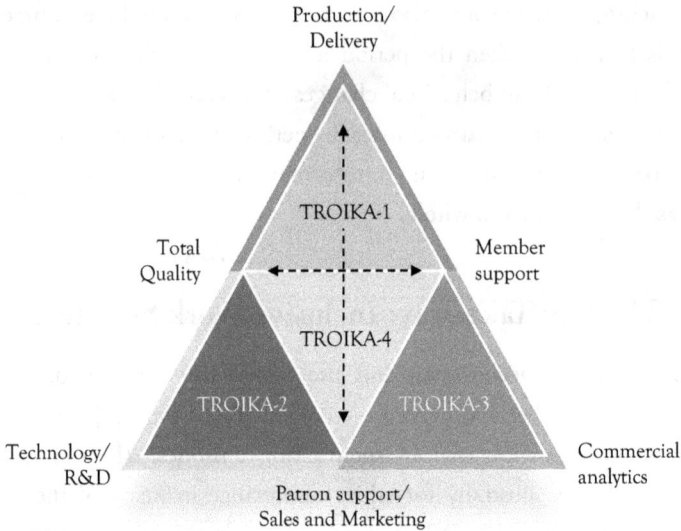

The *troika model* was the backbone of organization design
in successful business turnaround of two of the Chennai based
businesses with member count in excess of 7500 and 2000 respectively.

Figure 7.2 Troika work structure

and *patron support* is introduced to replace the commonly used exclusive expressions like *human resource management* and *customer support,* respectively, to steer clear of the overly transactional and material overtones of such phraseology, commonly used in contemporary management vocabulary. In the ethics–abundance framework, the individual actor is personally responsible for her goal of self-realization, and as a member of the overall business integer, she seeks support with fellow actors to combine in an inclusive and collective composition for the maturity of her individual business and personal goals.

CHAPTER 8

Quality Control Versus Quality Dharma

Subjective Cause and Objective Effect

There is no denying that subjective is the cause and objective is its effect. Although the idea of subjective is metaphorical, abstract, and at times, even mythical, it is indeed the reality-causing reality. Therefore, the treatment to be accorded to the subjective must be characteristically objective in the overall full-ness of the subjective–objective relationship, and not the subjective. It is a paradox that while the impersonation of objectivity is always controlled by subjectivity, subjectivity by itself must be meticulously managed with highly sanitized objectivity. The booby trap is no doubt the objectivity, but the devil laying the decoy is subjectivity. All decisions being taken by the business actor, without exception, are categorically subjective in the ultimate analysis—therefore, the subjective self of the business actor must be redeemed early. Quality of the internal decision support system of the business actor must be improved, first to last, to manifest the ethics–abundance dispensations from her. A tree's exterior is inherent in its seed's interior—this is the fundamental law of nature that cannot be ignored. Ethics–abundance values are to be installed right through the action episodes in the everyday work routine of the business actors. It should be indubitably clear that the objective quality is rooted in the subjective quality—the quality of actor's being—her essential being—her *dharma*. As explained in the preceding pages, the word *dharma* comes from the Sanskrit root—dhri, which means to hold or support. In Vedantic postulates, *dharma* is defined as the holding principle—we analogize this as the ethics–abundance principle—that supports the absolute essential being of man—the collective conscious of his integrated self. Everything in the bio-gaia system has its own *dharma* because it must rely on something for its existence—it is the essential nature of a thing or being, without which it cannot exist—for example, a fire burns because of its *dharma*—the power of burning. The *dharma* of a man, as we contend, is to evolve him from a level of individual fulfillment to a level of collective flourish. Therefore, the authentic construct of *quality control* is in *quality dharma* of the individual-actor.

The Dominion of Quality Dharma

In the dominion of subjectivity, the grip of obligation is determinately secured before the release of rights. Claims and retribution follow an unqualified fidelity to *dharma*, the holding—ethics–abundance—principle. If the duty to produce and sell good-quality product or service is fulfilled by the business actor, the right to value for money is axiomatically protected for the patron who sets the benchmark for *good* quality. The underlying stumbling blocks meddling with human excellence initiatives in businesses are invariably not the dearth of actor skills. For human excellence, the ethics–abundance roots of the business must be deep and widely spread out. Quality of products or services is dependent not so much on the *quality circles* or the *seven-step problem-solving process,* as on the quality of the member actors' mind behind such quality circles. Pareto charts, the five whys, fishbone diagrams, scatter diagrams, or failure mode effect analysis (FMEA) are all important as the cause analysis tools for efficient problem-solving. Nevertheless, an increasing dependence on tools and external gimmickry tend to cloak only the inner insufficiency and the needless keeps multiplying. Business actors then chase after them at ever-increasing greed–speed, often concealing the lack of internal competence.

Abundance Model of Quality Excellence

For excellence to be demonstrable, two major changes in the business actor's consciousness must superstruct—an experiential perception of the collective human flourish and a growing state of inner abundance. This is the substratal for *inner sustainability* of the unceasing human in a disposition in which all her disuniting and localized desires are effectively reigned in and *outer maintainability* of the persevering man in an application in which all his alienating and dispersed fears of failure are efficiently muted—gradually freeing him from the noumenal scarcity. Once these two vital transformations are initiated within the being of the business actor, an authentic foundation and integral power of the ethics–abundance inspiration will both have been laid firmly. Inadequate education of the manager actor in collective consciousness of human flourish has indeed increased the ethics–abundance value gaps that could be seen in display in her everyday work life—well-nigh cumbering her sensitivity to the internal actor's patronage. It is only through the service of internal patron actor—commonly referred to as internal customer—that the business system could serve the external patron—the internal delivers to the external. In the abundance consciousness, individual identity is subsumed in the collective identity—ordinate–personal goal is involved in the superordinate–collective goal. If this protocol of individuality–collectivity is assimilated, then the emphasis on personal rights and claims will be replaced by the stress on duties and obligations for the collective human flourish.

Total Quality Mind for Total Quality Management

Let us take our subjective–objective code a little further to discuss the hitherto well-established Total Quality Management (TQM) philosophy driving production or service organizations of most present-day businesses. And, because the subjective mind drives the objective action episodes, we could as well say, the subjective *total quality mind* (TQMs) drives the objective *total quality management* (TQMo). The principle thesis here is that TQMs is the cause and TQMo the effect. To glorify the effect, the commensurate cause must be strengthened and therefore, the actor's mind must be aligned to the abundance of collective consciousness—with the cause being secure and ethical, the effect will also be enduring and authentic. As the cosmic mind has caused the glorious cosmic creation—analogously, a lofty mind alone could cause the wholesome outcomes—the likes of collective human flourish.

In objective terms, quality is directly associated with the reliability of the production or service system. Every mathematical and statistical model deployed for production analyses is routinely configured–reconfigured to ensure the reliability of production processes and guarantee outcomes as intended. The basic approach of TQMo is to construct a business-wide framework to ensure reliability of production or service system to deliver outcomes as objectivized. And, while this approach pinafores, by and large, all prospects pertaining to the domain of the business–patron relationship, the veiled and vital aspect essential to sustainability and continuity of the bio-gaia system is in perpetuum missed out. Therefore, the TQMo approach to excellence, while being necessary, is inadequate by itself to produce sustainable quality in the holistic bio-gaia framework. The widespread experience shows that even the best and apparently *foolproof* TQMo systems could be subverted by inadequate minds operating with and within the business system itself.

It is verily in this sense that the highly objectivized ISO systems, spearheading the drive for TQMo in businesses, need to be probed more deeply, and by that, we mean subjectively. Although it was never the principal theme of ISO systems to take TQMo to the hitherto inhabited higher pedestal of TQMs, it has ironically tarnished somewhat the sheen of even TQMo by way of its largely checklist-oriented approach to establish production service reliability of the operations system. Therefore, it is a sort of retrograde movement as far as managing the reliability of production service system is concerned.

The Subjective TQM (TQMs)

Then, how do we construct our total quality mind or TQMs module that could drive TQMo and be institutionalized in the business system with greater reason to embrace the sustainability and continuity aspects of the holistic bio-gaia system? The answer to this could be offered in subjective and non-computable terms alone. At the very outset, it is, therefore, necessary to dispel a fairly common understanding among the statistical theorists that what is not measurable cannot be improved. On the contrary, most of human life provisos like humility, kindness, understanding, pain, fear, and many others are immeasurable, yet their materiality or substantiality needs no exemption. The business actor experiences them every day in her life. In fact, the very neglect of such immeasurable psychological conditions of everyday human life itself has allowed the intrinsic quality

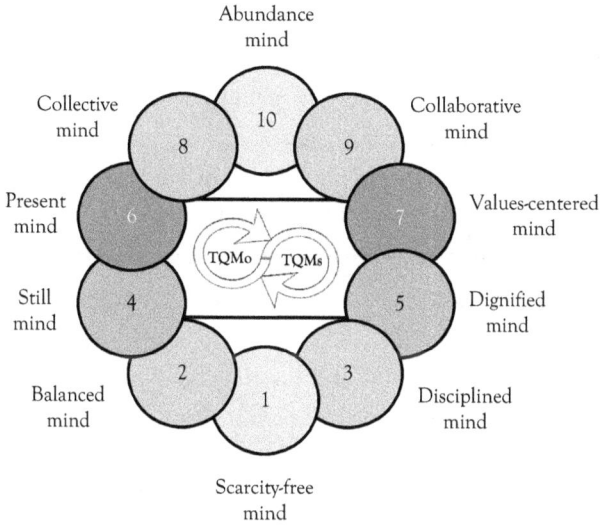

The actor-mind must be purified in the
mind sanitization sequence of TQMs for TQMo
to deliver sustained and holistic results.

Figure 8.1 The total quality mind (TQMs)

of human subjective existence to disintegrate beneath the complexity
of extrinsic objectivity. Having said that, let us list some of the key elements of TQMs that could admittedly be extracted from the subjective
deep structure of total quality mind of the fivefold human personality we
discussed earlier, see Figure 8.1.

1. A *scarcity-free* and emotionally unadorned mind that is beset in the
   live and let live predilection
2. An emotionally *balanced* mind that is in complete harmony with
   nature along the sustainability of the total bio-gaia system
3. A *disciplined* mind attuned to the leader–follower principle and
   anchored firmly in self-respect as well as obedience at the same time
4. A *still* mind that strives to maintain inner poise in success as well
   as failure—in approval as well as denial—to be cultivated by way
   of adopting the discipline of meditation on-the-go and regulating
   the breath
5. A *dignified* mind that is saturated with abundance and not scotched
   in the pettiness of scarcity–insecurity

6. A *present* mind that is past-free from the containments of the past and—future-free from the contingencies of the future
7. A *value-centered* mind that has renounced scarcity-driven pursuits for mundane individualistic gains
8. A *collective and humanized* mind on all five personality planes of the business actor (refer back to Figure 1.1)
9. A *collaborative and sharing* mind to neutralize the imprudent competitive biases in both conduct and actions of the business actor
10. The *abundance-filled* mind that fosters subjective inner affluence and contains no overtones of attachment owing to objective scarcity

These are, therefore, the ingredients of TQMs—largely absent in present-day business cultures—that could set a strong and worthy foundation for TQMo. A mind that sets itself on the TQMs track is less likely to deplete from scarcity-afflicted psychological entropy. It will be capable of nurturing a consciousness that could gradually move away from individual consciousness and empower itself through collective consciousness. The model remains valid as the grassroot framework of TQMs for business transcending cultures and geographies, simply because its roots are implanted in collective abundance of mind.

Revisiting Emotional Life Processes for TQMs

In the context of TQMs, we must, therefore, revisit the emotional life processes or, so to say, the emotional footings that make the business actor, a complete TQMs actor. These personality attributive emotions could underpin and guide her choices and decisions and direct her intellect or reason into her methods of execution and implementation of such choices and decisions. The human value set that the business pursues has a direct correlation with emotional conditioning of business actors' mind. In that sense, the reciprocation is not with the objectivized economic or technological value systems, but with subjective values of human beings devoid of pretensions, trump-ups, and insignia. The emotional life processes so conceived are sure enough critical for TQMs to progress on the advent to collective human excellence—collective human flourish. The grassroot expression of these collective emotions could be corroborated thus:

1. Affirming inclusivity as against assertive exclusivity conditioning
2. Caring relationship—between the business actor and her fellow actors as against individualistic–transactional relationship
3. Collaborative live and let live as against kill the competition stance
4. Collective self first as against individual self first inclination
5. Forget and forgive as against even-the-score attitude
6. I the collective actor as against me the individual actor mindset
7. Responsibility as against entitlement mind consciousness
8. Subjectively composed as against objectively aggressive mind state
9. True-to-need as against heed-the-greed orientation

Long-term and sustained campaign to cultivate and attune the mind with abundance conciousness is the basic and essential process for moving toward total quality mind.

Value, Policy, and Goals: Deploying the TQMs Way

Ethics–abundance values, the policies congruent with these values, and the goals—ordinate and superordinate—set forth along the value–policy lines, must all be taken together and deployed right across the business stratum and structure. It is only when the annual business plan is backwardly integrated with the ethics–abundance principle, the TQMs and thereby the TQMo could make any meaningful headway to deliver sustainable business results. We could adopt the well-known Hoshin Kanri X-Matrix template to deploy values, policies, and business goals to ensure that all the elements of the business plan are aligned and strengthened in the *total quality mind,* see Figure 8.2.

Once the goals are subjectively sanitized through the process of TQMs, the business actor is set to roll out the objective deployment of ordinate goals by way of TQMo. The subjective–objective interplay is, thus, completed, and TQMs is fully backing the TQMo.

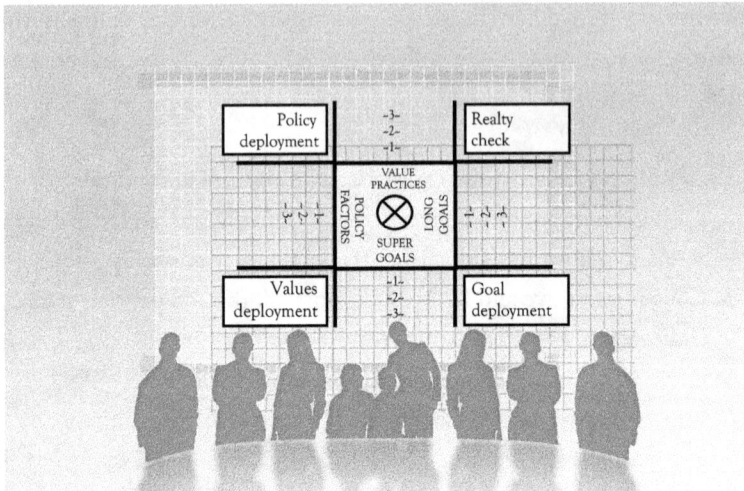

Hoshin Kanri X-Matrix could be used to deploy ethics–abundance sanitized values, policies, superordinate and ordinate goals.

Figure 8.2 *Values, policy, and goal deployment*

The Key Takeaway

The systems- and structures-driven TQMo efforts, though thorough and mathematical, lack the holistic perspective. Also, TQMo misses the essence of the cause–effect sequence, even though it sources its entire modus operandi from this very same principle. Quality is necessarily in the mind of the business actor. It originates in her subjective self. The more authentic and comprehensible the subjective self of the actor is in business, the better is the chance for TQMo to deliver sustainable and holistic outcomes, not only for the business actor as part, but the human actor as whole.

CHAPTER 9

Productivity Management Versus Productivity Karma

The Karma Doctrine

Although the abundance consciousness by itself is uncaused cosmic energy, the ethics–abundance bearing of human existence has an unflinching cause-and-effect sequence underlying it, just as every other phenomena of the physical world are governed by this very principle. The ethics–abundance world of the business actor is not even a bit arbitrary or fortuitous. Work life of the business actor could be effectively educated and managed to superior levels of existence. But for such an overruling principle, the very same life of the business actor could spiral down to inferior levels of human survival. In other words, each one of the business actors is an ethics–abundance reactionary with potential to either ascend or descend down the moral planes of human existence. What the business actor does as an act of karma in the bio-gaia or on the cognitive or intellectual plane has a corresponding relationship with her physical, emotional, as well as intellectual personality build-up. However, an instinctive action is not karma—that is akin to the pre-programmed existential action integrated in the gaia system itself and manages the sustenance of everything in nature—even animals, birds, and trees. So, karma is a discretionary or voluntary *action* and this might include *inaction*.

It is also important to understand the difference between karma and Newton's work—while action involves a force and the resultant displacement at physical level, karma involves an alert and silent contemplation of a problem at the cognitive level. The former is work in the domain of kinetic energy, while the latter is karma in the domain of potential energy. Regardless, both the *kinetic work* as well as *potential karma*, as discussed, are *karma* as long as they are volitional. Therefore, in a cause-and-effect relationship, the present being—or the circumstances thereof—of the business actor is the effect of her past karma. The mere knowledge and understanding of this causal relationship between karma and destiny could be leveraged by the business actor to alter and modify her being or the circumstances of being. As Ayn Rand, the Russian-American writer and philosopher said: "We can evade reality, but we cannot evade the consequences of evading reality." The business actor could ignore Newton, but not the gravitational law that necessarily impacts her life and existence—this is the doctrine of karma (DoK). Therefore, a correct understanding of DoK becomes an assured accentuation helping the business actor to become ever more aware. This is also one of the three processes of aligning the being of man with the collective ethics–abundance principle—the other two are through (holistic) knowledge and through love (for collective self), refer back Figure 2.1. It is also pertinent to comprehend that the basis of DoK is the ethics–abundance principle and not the desire-fulfillment accent of the emotional mind. Therefore, an ethical karma may or may not cause (fructify) the *desired* result—you can play a piano by way of knowing to play it, not by way of your desire to play it! Therefore, *ethics* cannot substitute for all the other inputs that must necessarily go into doing a *good* business!

Work Ethic and Ethics at Work

As we discussed, the attributes theory provides the insights into three major psychological urges of man—dynamic equilibrium (DE), stimulated entropy (SE), and chaotic inertia (CI)—that determine the ethical–unethical bias of the dynamic–active side of the human personality and her being. The DoK, as we discussed, provides the cause-and-effect framework as a supplementary system for the attribute-skewed actions. The detached karma code—karma that is psychologically detached from the outcome of the karma action—offers a psychological approach to work that can prevent unethical urges of the attribute-skewed personality of the business actor and, at the same time, spur the ethical elements embedded in her personality and the being. Simultaneously the three urge elements—DE, SE, and CI—construct a framework in which the business actor could perform detached work and desireless actions for productive—with minimum entropy—and ethically sound propitious effects, see Figure 9.1.

The subjective personality attributes of the business-actor
combine with her detached-karma to fine tune her focus
on the cause and not the effect and thereby
annex her work-ethic with ethics-at-work.

Figure 9.1 Work ethic and ethics at work

The ethical quality of a business actor's decisions tends to be compromised when her scarcity-driven individual self solicits desire fulfillment ($\bar{d}$) from work actions. Such individual-centric mooring could never be strong enough to support an actor's mind to establish the clear distinction between ethically right and wrong. This breeds inefficiency, as the flow of fulsome psychological energy—the cosmic abundance—is impaired. Desire-less action aligns readily with the ethics–abundance collective consciousness as opposed to individual consciousness. It also prevents the leakage of psychological energies through holes created by such desires in actor's cognitive personality that lowers her ability to carry out newer actions. The desire-less work action is, therefore, an attitude to work that could be cultivated and activated by the actor—as only humans possess such endowment and bounden subjective mooring. Once this psycho-frame of desire-less action is established in the business actor's cognitive personality, she acquires a natural spontaneity in her being like any other natural process in the bio-gaia system, and then, her work ethic could integrate freely with ethics at work.

Desire-less work means, work dedicated to work itself—and nothing else. If the actor only contemplates recompense to come forth from her hard work, then she is not truly committed to the work, she is only committed to returns. And, because the business is not likely to be in sympathy with actor-specific arithmetic and estimations, these recompenses could remain elusive for the business actor. It could, of course, be argued that remaining detached to the consequences of action could make the business actor non-committal and unaccountable to the work right at the outset. And, to answer to this, we need to go back to our arguments on *dharma*, the holding principle—work must be performed for the sake of doing it, to its true-ness and the effect of the cause should then follow along the unfailing ethics–abundance principle without the business actor waiting for the outcome. The actor is, thus, attached to the cause and not to the effect—this is detached attachment to work. Thus, the animative dynamism exuding from boisterous and efficiency-oriented mind may well produce a vigorous work ethic, yet this may not be propitious work for the collective and wholesome outcomes. Desire-less actions, by containing the $\bar{D}$-fulfillment agenda of the actor, could undeniably restore the natural rhythm to her work—and the business actor could in effect make choices in favor of collective self and common good. The business actor then works and acts in complete harmony with cosmic abundance.

High Entropy, Low Efficiency

To examine ethics at work from the leader-actor standpoint, we must clearly appreciate the fundamental distinction between self-actualization and self-realization. Leaders at the highest echelons, with all their lower-order needs satisfied, do often prattle their views in manners similar to anyone much lower in the Maslovian hierarchy. It means, ethics at work is beyond the sphere of self-actualization. The same work ethic plays up and down from lowest to the highest echelons of the hierarchy within the frame of the five-level Maslovian need hierarchy, or should we say, the contrive of greed hierarchy, refer back Figure 1.3. The argument goes like this—if business actor at any level in the self-actualization band mixes her actions drenched in unsavory experiences from the past with her contingencies for the future and the greed–speed work ethic in the present, the resultant space of work could only be overindulgent, impassioned, and unstable due to high entropy. The efficiency of the consequential servicing environment is bound to be low, see Figure 9.2.

The truth is, however, quite different as the human actor is already complete, and this completeness is to be just realized by the actor—she

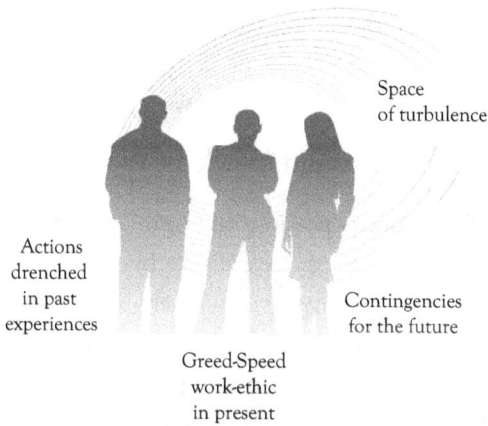

The greed-speed inflicted present is encroached by past experiences
and future contingencies and in effect turns into
turbulent space-time with high entropy and low efficiency.

Figure 9.2 *Space of high entropy–low efficiency*

just needs to transcend her mind–intellect domain and detach with all
lower-order attachments—she needs to self-realize, not self-actualize, and
then, ethics at work could naturally flow.

Service Through Ethics at Work

The basic theme of the ethics–abundance principle is oneness in
whole-ness. The business actor could fulfill her needs in a *live and let
live* frame of mind where personal needs are nay more important than
inter-personal needs. Therefore, *giving* becomes the key element of ethics
at work. In fact, giving is so 'natural' in nature that the business actor—
endowed with the additional reflective individual consciousness—some-
how tends to flout this precept and thereby introduces imbalance in her
entire work environment. And, because the business culture is also the
calling of the causal principle of giving, the depriving effect of *do not
return for what you get* results in the weakening of ethics at work. The
actor in business could display ethics at work only when her actions
are inspired by the humble feeling of an obligation to *give*, refer back
Figure 5.1. Freedom at work is not linked to rights and privileges attached
to the role the business actor plays, but to a constant awareness of

collective consciousness that all work done by her is to get freedom from this obligation. Ethics at work is, thus, triggered through the emotion of serving the collective human.

Excellence Through Work Is Worship

Objective excellence at work is possible only through subjective excellence within the business actor. And, excellence by itself must be redefined as, *going beyond the competitive exploits*—every business act could be managed, with some effort of course, through this subjective inspiration. *Cause and effect* is not an idea of passivity and predetermination. On the contrary, it places full accountability on the business actor for her actions. The business actor herself is the cause, and no one else—and she alone is responsible for the effects induced by her actions. And, this itself should be the all-powerful *incentive* for her to stay on the ethical track—a collective cause now in present must bring forth wholesome effect later in future. This effect may or may not fit into the scheme of the business actor's individual self, but certainly will be in consonance with human flourish in the collective self. To cultivate holistic and collective mental attitudes is to deliberately raise the contrary and opposite thoughts—the *thinking and counter-thinking (TcT)* methodology. If the business actor's actions are carefully processed through disciplined routine of TcT, many of ethical infringement in work life could be easily avoided.

Developing Business Goals

To begin a task with a dose of incredulity is probably passable, but to culminate it on the same note cannot be anything but a major setback—that is to say, incredulity as a means of reaching a faith may be good—but not otherwise. Although data and facts speak something important, they do not necessarily present the reality or truth wholly. Moreover, facts or data by themselves do not convey anything worthwhile, as they are dependent on the interpretation of the business actor's mind to try and construct, so to say, a subordinate reality or truth. While economical–commercial goals are important for the business, for goals to be sustainable and relevant for the collective actor, we need to go back inside from the outside—to the subjective actor from the objective actor. In his book, *First Things First (1994)*, Steven R. Covey has suggested going to the end state and coming back from there to organize commensurate actions. However, unless the end state is beyond the economistic finites, both goals and the correlated actions could remain in the domain of scarcity. As we discussed, the sequence of goal-setting must be thus: values, policies, superordinate goals, and the ordinate-economic goals, refer back Figure 8.2. Unless the goals are aligned right through with collective values and wholistic sustainability, the collective human flourish could remain far-fetched, and therefore, such goals could serve no real or ethical purpose.

It is also pertinent here to recall the four human personality motors—economic, empathy, balancing, and freedom, refer back Figure 2.3. Likewise, business goals must as well be congruent with four subgoals—economic, social, equity, and freedom—so fundamental to human life as such. Equity in conduct and actions is the causal variable, while economic means are the resultant value helping to fulfill need-based collective and emotional desires. All these put together in a cause–effect relationship culminates into the freedom of business actor from her limited individual self to the unlimited collective self. This is the unfettered expression of the business actor beyond the bounds of scarcity to the freedom of abundance where all her individual moorings are effectively diluted and dissolved. Thus, equity, the upholding and bonding force is at the base and freedom is at the apogee—phased across the life span of the business actor. This is strategic management of actor-self along the deed and need hierarchy as against the greed hierarchy. Freedom and abundance are, thus, not the terminal states—rather, they are the destination states of collective human flourish.

The Productivity Karma

Having discussed the amalgamation of work ethic and ethic at work, let us now examine the karmic character of *productivity*, the spin-off of this co-action. In this sense, the productivity must necessarily be put against the wider perspective of a viable bio-gaia management strategy. All the competitive economic compulsions must go through the scrutiny of bio-gaia sustainability. In classical industrial engineering, however, productivity represents the search for more output, with either given inputs or relatively lower inputs per unit of output. This definition of productivity suites the standard narrative of the businesses that more output from production must lead to higher standard of living for business actors. But, there lies the underlying inconsistency as *higher standard of living,* the subjective aspiration of the business actor could not be linked to *higher standard of consumption,* promised by the instrumental productivity by way of *higher output*—the no-holds-barred objective phenomenon subjected to greed–speed dynamics, as we discussed. And, greed–speed hides away the entire spectrum of business motives from more and more material power to a heady dominion power. In the bargain, the gaia system undergoes deterioration and decay. In the holistic frame of bio-gaia sustainability, therefore, the idea of productivity must also undergo transformation. Sheer compulsions of a flourishing human existence could affirmatively enforce this change.

The business actor then, instead of production, must focus on improved conservation of *given* inputs and better distribution of *lesser* outputs. The new measures of values-driven bio-gaia conservation and distribution of production output must, therefore, be evolved. The predominant objective and instrumental view of industrial engineering and production–productivity must accommodate this indispensable subjective change. The role of technology is equally important in leading this change. The current efforts of technology to improve the input–output ratio in objective terms need to be enhanced significantly to cover the subjective and the larger bio-gaia framework. Businesses must move from *desire* to *need.* The key input to *productivity karma* should be the *collective perspective.* And wherever this productivity karma is directed, the assured output will certainly be *collective abundance.* The collective perspective thus implies, see Figure 9.3:

- A mind sensitized to bio-gaia existence—meaning less on grabbing and more on giving
- A lever of constancy amidst the shrinking present—meaning low on greed–speed
- An expansive and inclusive consciousness—meaning restrained pettiness and fortified dignity

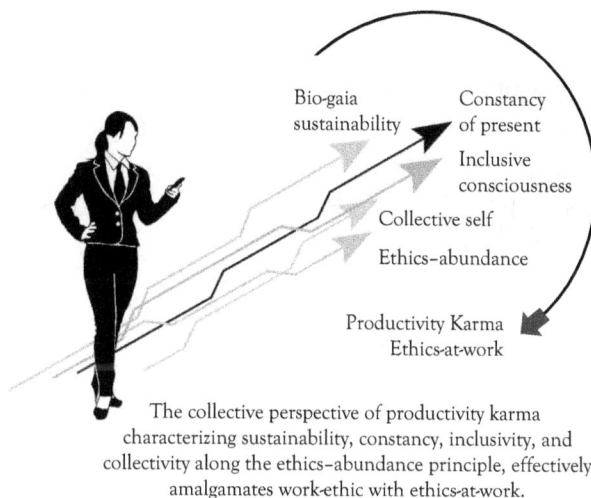

Bio-gaia
sustainability

Constancy
of present

Inclusive
consciousness

Collective self

Ethics–abundance

Productivity Karma
Ethics-at-work

The collective perspective of productivity karma
characterizing sustainability, constancy, inclusivity, and
collectivity along the ethics–abundance principle, effectively
amalgamates work-ethic with ethics-at-work.

Figure 9.3 The collective perspective and productivity karma

- A secure mind that connects with the collective self
- An intellect aligned to ethics–abundance principle

In the productivity karma consciousness, the business actor, over a period of time through systematic total quality management (TQM) practice, is more likely to become an effective and ethical processor of abundance, the cosmic energy—productivity is effective energy processing after all! The intangible energy is what precipitates into tangible matter. Although, all effort toward exalted productivity karma must eventually find expression at the individual actor level as well as the collective business level, a systematic transformation of the lower-order greed–speed afflicted actor mind is a prerequisite for progressively attaining the unitive collective consciousness. And, from the global business perspective as well, the idea of productivity must take measure of bio-gaia sustainably. The poor *objective* productivity ethic is fundamentally an ethics–abundance dilution-related issue—therefore, the sustainable *subjective* productivity karma could be the only way to go into a sustainable bio-gaia order. The vigor of productivity karma must be brought right into the middle of all productivity management plans and actions—and, the real purpose of this crucial intervention in operations or production management is to reconcile and optimize the material needs of businesses for a sustainable bio-gaia existence of the collective human.

The Key Takeaway

The very nature of bio-gaia existence is the duality of opposites—every action, every phenomenon, and every thought has an equally strong counterpart lurking from the opposing end—this is an unavoidable physical law. No work is free from this, so to say, it is a peculiarity of the nature. So, the only way to remain balanced in the midst of this interplay of duality is to amalgamate individual work ethic with ethics at work—and this is not about acquiring a new skill or technique—it is to cultivate the mind to rise above the objective and individual-centric gains to the subjective state of collective gains within the bounds of bio-gaia sustainability. This is the holistic theory of work and essence of productivity karma. The duty-oriented work ethic must blend with ethics at work—rights will automatically follow, as duty is the cause and right is the effect.

CHAPTER 10

The Hundred-Year Organization

Let us now discern and aggregate the unembellished essential ideas from what we have discussed in the previous nine chapters. All things considered; it is now amply clear that the ethics–abundance principle of causation governs the entire human existence. In effect, this is the counterpart of the cosmic law of order embedded in all affairs of human beings and every human act and thought has an ethics–abundance dimension. An act in the present will inescapably produce a corresponding effect in the future. A business actor—by effecting her thoughts and actions—inexorably sets a perpetual cause–effect chain into motion during the course of her lifetime. The unfulfilled desires ($\bar{d}$ or $\bar{D}$) and the unbroken cause–effect chains constitute the causal force for the next phase of her existence in the perennial life cycle (PLC) sequence of the collective human and continues with the unfinished process of $\bar{d}$-fulfillment. The PLC sequence, therefore, offers a long-term and purposed view of collective human existence. Instead of predestinarian torpidity, it promotes an active sense of exclusive responsibility and accountability for the individual actor to transform her life. The human actor, therefore, creates her own destiny—present from the past and future from the present. This lays the foundation of the *hundred-year organization* springing forth from the *thousand-year conformation* of collective human constancy and permanence.

In the PLC sequence there are, in all, just two fields of action for the human actor—the business composition and family disposition and the approach for her transformation could either be objective or subjective, whether in family or in business regulation. Let us, therefore, recapitulate our conversance and the yin–yang of these two existential versions of transformation—subjective and the objective:

- The basis of the objective approach is reason and analysis through the mind–intellect instrument in which the problem is typically placed outside of the collective self. The temporal dominion becomes the governing principle here, and the process of managing is essentially mechanical.
- However, the subjective approach is intuitive and proceeds from beyond the mind–intellect domain, and the governing principle is the unitive ethics–abundance principle within the collective self. The fundamental goal here is self-realization, as against self-actualization, in the objective approach.

Based on the preceding distinction, it is evidently clear that the qualitative and quantitative dimensions of a business actor's existence is an effect, which is the projection of her internal subjective self as the cause in a *so the subject so the object* normality. Therefore, the conventional *managing by objectives* (MBO) paradigm could yield results—qualitative and quantitative—only to the extent of how the business actor manages her subjective self by way of *managing by ethics* (MBE). While MBO could potentially be a rational, disciplined, as well as a collaborative process in a given situation, the conclusive outcomes resulting from it could only be subordinate to the quality of MBE. And, like the duality of objectivity–subjectivity in human life, managing business is also an interplay of MBO–MBE in tandem, see Figure 10.1.

Transforming Work Ethos: Managing by Ethics

As we discussed, human values are congenital in the business actor's subjective self, and therefore, her ethical leanings will have unavoidable and potent influence over the plans and goals she devises for the business. In the final analysis, bumbershoot business values always derive from the underlying values of its actors. While the method to a work could bank on the tools and techniques deployed, the method to approach the human side of the business hinges on the collective and individual values of the business actors. The business actor's action could be deemed ethical and long-standing only if her abundance consciousness is expressed through it, and this is what MBE means. The businesses cannot escape

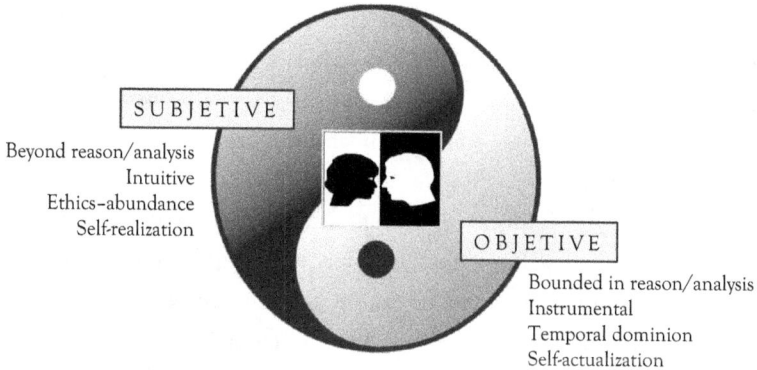

SUBJETIVE

Beyond reason/analysis
Intuitive
Ethics–abundance
Self-realization

OBJETIVE

Bounded in reason/analysis
Instrumental
Temporal dominion
Self-actualization

Managing by ethics is the interplay
of man's subjective and objective dimensions.

Figure 10.1 MBO and MBE

engagement with the ethics–abundance values within the actor's being—
ethics at work flows from values in being. These values within the business
actor's subjective self configure her mind and guide her actions either
for the collective or the individual good. Ethics–abundance relate to the
business actor's subjective self and also forms the basis for trust in all her
human–business relationships.

The near-pandemic fallout of scientific management theories has been
fuel to the business actor's highly stimulated greed–speed objectivity. While
objectivity by itself is not an inequity, overemphasis on tools and techniques has undeniably increased the noncomposure between objective and
subjective. Ethics–abundance values cannot sprout and grow unless there
is natural rhythm established in the business actor's exteriorized–interior-
ized coexistence. In other words, everyday work discipline and balancing
of work life are inescapable—you may recall our discussion on PPF motor
here. In operational sense, therefore, disciplined behavior does result in
a positive attitude and ethics–abundance value formation. The subjective–objective has an infallible reciprocal relationship in which the ethics–
abundance values shape the behavior of the business actor, and in turn,
her behavior replenishes her values. Therefore, the culture-building efforts
through practices and observance in businesses should reflect this inducible
aspect, as the illustrative philosophy and the guiding ethics–abundance
values of the business are embedded in such practices and observance.

A business is the effect, and the business actor is its cause—and it should not be mistaken the other way round. The business actor owns personal responsibility for her value orientation and behavioral transformation in order to leave behind an ethics–abundance sound business endowment behind her for posterity.

Evidently, the business in present times wrests with an array of global crises ranging from increasing inequality and poverty to terrorism and pandemics—to mass migration and environmental extermination—and all of them further amplified by climatic nullification. The bio-gaia injury–abuse is one of the most obvious worriment for MBO as humanity, to satisfy her ever-increasing desires, is consuming far in excess of the reproductive capacity of the system. The panoptic economy uses more resources than could be replenished commensurately, leading to an unstable growth and increasingly frequent economic effervesce. Shareholder value and economic–commercial chauvinism is plundering, rather than preserving value for the future. MBO focuses on yield maximization at the business level, and wage–dividend growth at business actor level—all in all, this is the objective–materialistic view to gratify the individual being and not the sparing–restraining view for flourish of the collective being.

MBO in effect holds the narration that business actors are fundamentally self-indulgent and continually looking for material accomplishments as the meter of success. In more objective terms, these assumptions refer to business actors as individuals driven by rational interests aimed at maximizing utility. And, in unerring terms, gains–income has gradually superseded as a broad concept of what measures out as bona fide *happiness*. The quantity of *options* has, thus, superseded the quality of *futures*. And while the economic–commercial behavior of business actors could be studied in a market setting where price mechanism regulates the supply–demand dynamic for the product–service, such considerations awfully lack in capturing the bio-gaia complexities as a whole.

The basic motif of MBO is scarcity, and therefore, yield maximization becomes the predict of effectiveness. The chosen operating theme of business is accelerated efficiency. Efficiency is further classified in more objective and utilitarian terms such as massively favorable cost–benefit ratios. In this stark–bare framework, the business actors become resources as in *human resource,* and qualitative assessment gets replaced with quantitative evidence. Frederic Taylor first heralded such a perspective through the postulates of his *Scientific Management Theory* in 1909, and many, since then, adopted it with edacious perseverance and the initial success of businesses almost legitimized the expediency of the dominant Taylorism. But, per contra regrettably, the Taylorian understanding of scientific management has violated both the uncaused and caused aspects of human dignity by treating business actors like machines and preventing their material and non-material development by way of assigning their movements as mere therbligs. Imprudently, the Taylorian scientific management tradition is visible inordinately for so long in operations management, operations research, information systems, as well as in strategic management, organizational behavior, and marketing in businesses across the terrene.

From the MBO perspective, markets dictate the terms of business and coordinate backward with business actors to work out the admissible utility maximization strategies and programs. In this, businesses compete against one another to gratify just the markets. Only when markets fail to deliver the expected bottom-line scores—as knee-jerk response—businesses turn to some semblance of collaboration, teamwork, rationalistic objectivity, and the likes to anywise emerge out of such self-spawned crises. The MBE perspective, on the other hand, suggests that organizations could be better seen as collaborative cooperatives. This, therefore, transcends the MBO perspective of organizations as rigid dominions or market-based set of business contracts. MBE views business as an existential phenomenon essential to the business actor, the indubitable relational being. Therefore, businesses could tread beyond quantitative parameters and embrace a balance of qualitatively desirable outcomes as well. These businesses then mutually collaborate with all the stakeholders, including corresponding or so-called competitive businesses in same market space. The MBE businesses balance their goals and objectives rather than maximize any particular objective. The ubiquitous ambition of collective good requires that multiple objectives be integrated and harmonized to create a shared value for all the stakeholders in business.

The foundation of MBE is deep-laced in ethics–abundance within the carrying capacity of the bio-gaia system and inevitably protects the dignity and self-respect of the business actor to the promotion of collective well-being, rather than pettiness and self-indulgence to accelerate her greed–speed propensities. The abundance perspective allow the leader actors to understand the importance of care, grasp the notion of human dignity, and organize business actors toward a superordinate goal beyond the ordinates of economic–commercial mechanisms. The four elemental functions of managing business in MBO—planning, organizing, leading, and controlling (P-O-L-C) then gets modified as—planning, organizing, leading and sustaining (P-O-L-S) in the MBE perspective—this is the essence.

Planning (-P-): The Common Minimum Program

In the operational sense, all business initiatives must be guided through a common minimum program (CMP) pivoted to collective abundance consciousness, which, as we discussed, has the five-fold being character— it is self-sustained, it is self-aware, it is infinite, it is collective, and it is integrative. In the functional apprehend, the CMP, so-collated could be affirmed as *operative subprinciples of the abundance consciousness,* see Figure 10.2:

1. *Bio-gaia sustenance principle* coming from the self-sustaining charac-teristic of abundance consciousness
2. *Mentor–mentee principle* coming from the self-awareness and self-learning characteristics of abundance consciousness
3. *Time principle* that explains the manifested humanity as continuum in infinity
4. *Interdependency principle* that places the interdependent human in the collective relationship frame
5. *Coexistence principle* that integrates man with all other things and beings in the bio-gaia system

The operative CMP in the frame of the so-constructed five sub-principles must, therefore, guide all actions of the business actor in her everyday life. Ethics–abundance values should then fall into their nat-ural place within the holistic and collective frame. Usual systems and

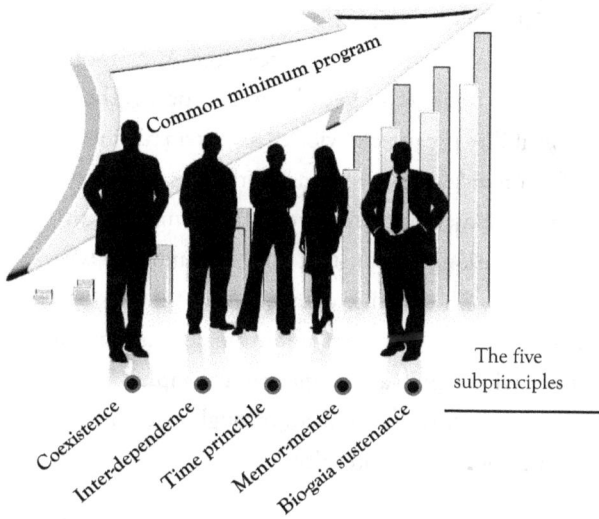

The common minimum program in the frame of
five subprinciples of ethics–abundance consciousness.

Figure 10.2 The common minimum program

structures within the business, however, need to support the CMP framework to establish requisite checks and balances.

MBE is, thus, the subjective foundation for MBO or similar analytical and scientific management tools to yield holistic and bio-gaia sustainable business outcomes. However, MBE remains culture-specific at operating levels, although the underlying tone could certainly be all-embracing and collective. Therefore, unlike technology, which could move across the meridian uni-facially, the methods for MBE, essentially being an experiential process, mandates a unique culture-centric treatment. In admittance of the CMP, therefore, there are three aspects to human values that we need to elaborate—only all-inclusive and trans-cultural human values could be the ideals—culture-specific operative human values that translate the ideals into actionable conduct in each culture must be identified and assimilated and—the culture-specific operative human values that derive from certain altogether different ideals must also be thought about and included in the CMP.

The main function of a MBO organization is to maximize and gather material affluence, allowing individual actors to pursue individualistic privileges and entitlements (recall the ACC motor function we discussed) within their respective utility functions. Therefore, the individual responsibility is generally viewed as systematic interference to their freedom. The organizational responsibilities are only heeded when they are expressly mandated and are part of the dominion infrastructure. In the MBE organization, the constant ethics–abundance is connected with the responsibilities for systemic consequence of individual actions. And, individual freedom is contingent upon the conduct of individual actor in conformity with ethics–abundance subprinciples. The individual and collective freedom, thus, materializes through care and concern for each other in the business actor fraternity.

Organizing(-O-): End-State Values and Values as Means

Then the end-state values, like productivity, profitability, market share, innovation, growth, and the like, and values as means must be made analogous, as the abundance stance through values as means alone could characterize the end-state values as sustainable and collective. The method to achieve what is valued is equally important as what is valued, and therefore, the ethics–abundance values sensitization, as we discussed, becomes extremely crucial to the business goals deployment process. Fulfillment of short-term objectives must be congruent with long-term ordinate and superordinate goals. Efficiency, proficiency, and work design and their sequencing are the objective parameters of work, while the ethics–abundance values must be the subjective basis of work—subjective is the cause and objective is the effect. Subjects like leadership, communication, interpersonal relations, and the like come under the domain of the ethics–abundance principle. Therefore, the long-term effectiveness of the CMP depends equally, if not more, on the practice of sound human values in the following arrangement:

1. The process must begin with each individual actor
2. A great deal of *surplus* in skills cannot balance out *void* in values

3. Values are *to be,* while skills are *to do*

4. Even strong skills coupled with weak values induce work life depreciation

5. Value as means require a deep understanding of what makes the business actor integrated and stable within herself

MBO businesses support individual-centric cultures and organizational identities, which are transactional in nature. Consequently, interaction processes within an organization are mechanistic and the closed-loop. On the contrary, organizational practices are inclusive, participative, and value-based in MBE businesses. They foster constant dialog between the actors in business, and therefore, the culture is transformational in nature, and organizational identities are based on collective interpersonal relations. The individual actor because of her indivisible connect with the collective actor is placed determinedly in the very middle of the MBE structure—breach of this ethical basis is considered a breach of fundamental unity ingrained in abundance. Therefore, *respect for individual* and *mutual cooperation* are aspiration of all interpersonal relationship in the business ecosystem. Quality of what is done is primarily a function of the quality of mind and the consciousness of the business actor. Therefore, work must be aligned firmly with the time-honored ethics–abundance principle in terms of containing greed–speed and reinforcing self-discipline, self-restrain, and detached attachment to focus on action and defocus on outcomes—thereby conserve the psychological energies of the business actor. The end-result values could only be attained through values in means, and the idea of work cannot, therefore, remain void of collective ideals.

Leading (-L-): The MBE Leadership

The girth of MBE is abundance, and its operative basis is the ethics–abundance principle—the cosmic order. Therefore, intuitive "seeing and believing" of abundance and the cosmic order must be the fundamental goal of the MBE leader. The leader actor is, thus, an agent of this cosmic order to galvanize and align the entire leadership process to the ethics–abundance principle. Once the leader actor operates in this collective principle, the leadership process will naturally be ethical and honorable. It is this ethics–abundance that holds the redeeming answer to uphold human dignity, and the glory of gaia in entirety must, therefore, be captured by the leader actors followed by the follower actors. Mind and intellect will have their instrumental roles at all times no doubt, but the original drive and impulse will necessarily flow from the illumined intuitions of the ethics–abundance principle.

The basis of MBE leadership is then refined in the capacity to refer the fluctuating individual self to the constant collective, self established in coexistence, all-embracing sustainability, and human flourish—materially and ethically. The transformed MBE leader will devote her life energies first in realizing this cosmic order of abundance herself, and then, to support the business as a whole in translating as much of this knowledge into business goals' actions as would be optimal for a healthy balance between the subjective and objective life of all the fellow actors. The business in MBE leadership is able to create a purpose beyond the economic–commercial profits and establish interpersonal relationships based on trust with various stakeholders and collaboration partners. To establish common goals, MBE businesses use discourse-based social processes wherein the leader is a mentor, rather than an appurtenance in hierarchical command-and-control mechanism.

MBO leaders, on the other hand, focus primarily on economic maximization and competitiveness. There is no place for leadership in the MBO framework, as all the business actors make decisions based on market commercialism. This is the present-day hierarchy-less organization—the ineligible result of unduly stretched market fixate. In an even deeper MBO view, the business is seen as a chain of commercial contracts that must be continuously negotiated. As a result, a MBO leader has to constantly negotiate on behalf of the business. In this sense, the MBO leader is essentially a hailer, whose task is to clarify the commercial goals and desired outcomes to fulfill the dictates of contracts with the follower actors to secure strict compliance from them and also set an objectivized incentive scheme plan to ensure the follower actors deliver as desired. Nurturing long-term relationships is rather irrelevant and often seen as hindrance to business interests of the organization. The practice of hire-and-fire requires MBO leaders to be emotionally disconnected from the follower actors who are simply considered as human resource, and the skillful MBO leader is finally the one who is expected to maximize the efficiencies.

Sustaining (-S-): The Governance Practices

Getting exclusive access to information, the primary goal of a top-down governance structure in the MBO is to control the business actors to fulfill their business objectives with singular focus on efficiency. The MBO decision-making process begins by identifying a problem, then defining the decision criteria, allocating weights to the criteria, developing alternatives, evaluating alternatives, and finally, selecting the best alternative. However, the *control* function suffers a basic lacuna, essentially that humans have limited ability to receive, store, process, retrieve, and transmit information. Consequently, the leadership is frequently confronted with a difficult task of sustaining the command-and-control-based business structure. An added and key element of establishing control in MBO business is based on monetary incentive systems. Such incentive systems are considered the central control element to align diverging interests of the individual business actors to the desired business outcomes. And, such an idea of motivation goes well with the scarcity mind of business actors with virtually insatiable desires. The incentives, therefore, are considered the oft-accepted instruments to drive behavior change in them.

In a MBE business, however, the mentor–mentee principle assumes the higher-order self-realization (the IEE motor function) as the superordinate goal for all business actors to be approached by way of establishing bio-gaia (the PPF motor function) sustenance and drive the intrinsically inspired business actors to a higher level of commitment to total value creation in the business. While the top-down control mechanisms of MBO are essential for the administrative structure, checks and balance systems are the essential features in the MBE design. The *control-point and check-point* methodology, most commonly used as a tool in total quality management (TQM) practice, is the statistical version of the *checks and balance* system. When there are internal checks and balances, they mutually reinforce each other to serve various stakeholder actors' needs in a rather balanced way. MBE also rejects the idea that the business actors could be manipulated with carrots and sticks or, rewards and punishments—in the MBE perspective, the carrot is replaced with dignity. When something is part of a trade-off, it follows the mechanistic logic of *your desire versus my desire* and therefore is seldom found effective. Since the inception of one of Union Carbide's factories in India, the production actors did not push to earn incentive for 10 years, but once they were more closely involved in matters concerning their everyday work life, they achieved efficiency levels beyond 90 percent and earned handsome amount of incentives as well. This is the influence of dignity. In the MBE system, dignity—the uncaused natural effulgence by way of business actor's alignment with the ethics–abundance principle as well as the caused brilliance by way of her own actions is the critical basis for business sustenance, because it clearly approves that the individual actor is not a mere tool or resource, but a being with intrinsic worth.

As a cautionary note, however, it must be clarified here that dignity is not power or position. It is not meant to carve out any special treatment for the individual actor. It cannot be used as a subversive device or any guiding practice to establish equality or individual autonomy. Nevertheless, dignity could be ever so useful in conflict resolution as a pathway to forgiveness. It could also be particularly helpful in business actor's journey from individual self to collective self because the root of any conflict is the idea of separateness— therefore reconnecting the concept of dignity to a time-honored ethics–abundance principle addresses even the passing ambiguity about it.

MBE business has serial leadership–mentorship and period leaders–mentors who celebrate the big–small achievements of mentee actors in everyday work life upholding their dignity. They listen to them as every business actor matters in the total scheme of business. The prime focus of MBE is the holistic sustenance of the entire business ecosystem within the all-embracing sustenance of the bio-gaia system—suitable structures are built to foster mutual trust (the CRR motor function) and to build capabilities rather than to set up controls. The decision rights are spread throughout the organization in a way that utilizes the collective expertise of business actors. Jan Carlzon, the Swedish businessman and author of the book, *Moments of Truth (1985)*, did vest authority with his frontline airline staff working in the midst of everyday moments of truth with the airline's customers.

MBE governance structures could, therefore, be purposefully built to support a balanced growth of business actors in the all-inclusive bio-gaia sustainability framework. The ACE needs (the ACC motor function)—both tangible and intangible, could, therefore, be addressed through a self-assessment process in a mentor–mentee arrangement that allows for accountability and, at the same time, provides feedback system to make timely course corrections. The CRR needs of the actors could be addressed by way of providing a continuous learning experience to them and allow for creativity, experimentation, and continuous improvement to build a strong organizational culture based on mutual trust and obligation to serve each other in the spirit of mutual service.

On to the Recovery Path: The Ethics Paradigm and MBE Framework

As Max Weber (1864–1920), the German sociologist, philosopher, jurist, and political economist, opined, social science depends on the construction of abstract and hypothetical concepts. The Carnot Cycle is also a theoretical ideal thermodynamic cycle proposed by the French physicist Sadi Carnot in 1824. In a similar vein, therefore, the ideal of abundance could by all means germinate, cultivate, and eventually establish the ethics–abundance ideology toward the resurrection and revitalization of global business and the ultimate human flourish in a self-sustained human–nature coexistence. The starting point on the road to the recovery of ethics–abundance standards cannot be anything other than the following two convictions:

- Businesses must succeed even in competitive environments but with higher degrees of rectitude in ethics–abundance.
- That business actors, bar none, are as much a cause as an effect of the quality of business environment in which they function.

In the MBE framework, see Figure 10.3, the panoptic three balancing factors are thus:

1. The bio-gaia balance at the physical existence level;
2. The cognitive balance at emotional level and;

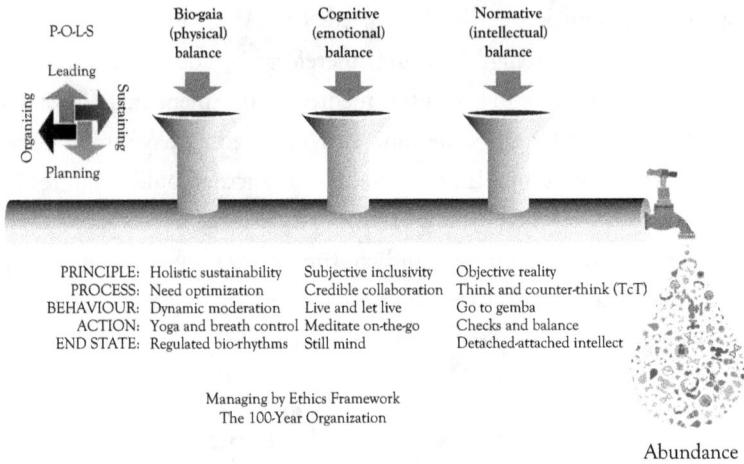

PRINCIPLE:	Holistic sustainability	Subjective inclusivity	Objective reality
PROCESS:	Need optimization	Credible collaboration	Think and counter-think (TcT)
BEHAVIOUR:	Dynamic moderation	Live and let live	Go to gemba
ACTION:	Yoga and breath control	Meditate on-the-go	Checks and balance
END STATE:	Regulated bio-rhythms	Still mind	Detached-attached intellect

Managing by Ethics Framework
The 100-Year Organization

Abundance

Figure 10.3 Managing by ethics framework

3. Normative balance at the intellectual level, for a completely balanced and integrated human actor personality. The operating principles at the three balancing levels are: a) holistic sustainability at the bio-gaia plane, b) subjective inclusivity in the way business actors relate with each other and gaia-system on the emotional plane, and c) objective reality to directly see and experience reality as truth beyond interpreted facts and beliefs deep seated in the realm of emotional mind on the intellectual plane. In the modified process schema of P-O-L-S—as against the ubiquitous P-O-L-C—the focus at the three levels of existence is: a) to optimize needs on the objective plane, b) to establish credible collaboration on the emotional plane, and c) to think and counter-think (TcT) on intellectual plane. The *counter point-of-view* lurking behind in the mind must be pulled into the frame of reference and be confronted with the *point of view*, to finally evaluate the options—for there cannot be thought without a counter-thought lurking at the same time in the mind. The manifested behavior at the three levels will, thus, be: a) dynamic moderation on the physical level, b) the live and let live attitude on the emotional level, and c) go-to-gemba (the Japanese term meaning the *actual place* or the *shop floor*) stance on the intellectual level. So, the basic idea here is to pick the real understanding and not the interpreted

misunderstanding. The three levels of actions will, therefore, be: a) manage breath through yoga or similar such practices as breath alone links man's physical personality with the rest of his personalities—emotional and intellectual, b) meditate on-the-go to balance the mind, and c) establish checks and balance to set right the deviations from the ethical path. And, the end state in the MBE framework on the respective three levels will be: a) a fully regulated bio-rhythmic body, b) a still mind, and c) a detached intellect— all set to see the truth and feel the infinite abundance within the consciousness of actor.

The Key Takeaway

A vision by and of itself should cause expediency and ascendancy—not the other way round. Self-realization through self-expediency is a gradual process—no one could change overnight! However, the first few steps— as we describe next—in the right direction could go a long way to construct the solid foundation for an MBE business:

1. Focus on long-term vision, products, and services, as against ever-shorter ones in present times—the short term is highly likely to be short lived.
2. Businesses should tend to collaborate and grow rather than compete and widen, as is the present thrust. The member–patron relations in the business should be less exclusive and more inclusive, irrespective of the size of business.
3. Localized and decentralized economic–commercial activities should increase faster than the centralized ones. Production and distribution should be more space- and time-specific and as Prime Minister Narendra Modi of India asserts, "vocal for local" must be the de novo and *big picture* global business mantra—and, businesses across-the-board must carry the respective local identity in the widest possible collective coexistence sense of this proposition.
4. The business actor in business could be the most authentic brand ambassador for the respective businesses—this intellection could

undeniably be explored, developed, and methodically instituted. The focus must be on business actors, bio-gaia fidelity, and products–services in that order. Business patrons would naturally be *happy* if the business actors are *delighted*—business actors cannot and should not be bypassed. A business patron could be a God, but certainly not the king—serve the *God* with love and faithfulness and not fear—as fear could only rob business actor of her dignity and preserve in freedom!

5. The sustainability of human–nature or the bio-gaia coexistence cannot be ignored at any time—the devastating results of such follies could be seen from time to time in epoch. A good economic–commercial sense must also be accompanied with an extremely caring bio-gaia sense. The time for entitlements and control should, for long, be over, as perenniality is the sustainability of man in nature, man in human, and in conclusion, human in humanity.

References

Carlzon, J. 1989. *Moments of Truth: New Strategies for Today's Customer Driven Economy*. New York: Harper Business.

Chakraborty, S.K. 2001. *The Management and Ethics Omnibus: Management by Values, Ethics in Management, Values and Ethics for Organizations*. New Delhi: Oxford University Press.

Govindarajan, V. 2016. *The Three-Box Solution: A Strategy for Leading Innovation*. USA: Harvard Business School Publishing.

Parthasarathy, A. 1978. *Vedanta Treatise*. India: A. Parthasarathy.

Pirson, M. 2017. *Humanistic Management: Protecting Dignity and Promoting Well-Being*. United Kingdom: Cambridge University Press.

Rosa, H., Translated by J.C. Wagner. 2019. *Resonance: A Sociology of Our Relationship to the World*. UK, USA: Polity Press.

Rosa, H., Translated by J. Trejo-Mathys. 2015. *Social Acceleration: A New Theory of Modernity*. New York: Columbia University Press.

About the Authors

Pradeep Nevatia, scd

Lost and found by his mother in the streets of Kolkata and nurtured by a no-nonsense upbringing, Pradeep grew up to be a man in search of himself. Stability, and yet exploration dominated his way of functioning throughout his professional career spanning 35 years across far-flung geographies, contrasting industries, and extensive hierarchies—roles. Pradeep, a pioneer of the rural BPO & CSR BPO business models in India and a former CEO is an acknowledged business turnaround expert. He has earned degrees in mechanical and industrial engineering from Birla Institute of Technology, Mesra, and NITIE, Mumbai. Pradeep's interests include concept astrology, playing piano, and thought photography. He lives with his family adorned with the two grandkids in Kolkata, India, and New York, United States.

Rahul Nevatia

Driven by an ambition to fly to the moon, Rahul pursued an education in rocket science. But, *9/11* had made such of his dreams much harder to pursue. He then retooled himself for a career on Wall Street where his risk-free–risk-taking mind could work predisposed to everyday rigmarole of financial markets. Rahul had stints with J P Morgan and Goldman Sachs in New York before bootstrapping his professional campaign from the high seas of hedge funds. The global financial crisis of 2008–2009 brutally sensitized him to business ethics... after all, the material dimension of ethics is embodied in pecuniary stratagem. Rahul has earned degrees in aerospace, mechanical, and financial engineering from the University of Michigan, Ann Arbor, and Cornell University. Rahul has also attended the Tuck Business Bridge Program at Dartmouth College. Rahul is a self-indulgent epicurean who loves exploratory travel. He lives with his family in New York, United States.

Index

www.ingramcontent.com/pod-product-compliance
Lightning Source LLC
Chambersburg PA
CBHW061314220326
41599CB00026B/4881